The Bottom Line

A Management Primer for First Line Law Enforcement Supervisors

by

Arthur Meister

TELEMACHUS PRESS

Cover designed by Telemachus Press, LLC

Cover art:
Copyright © iStock 679579_Medium_navid
Copyright © iStock 24190767_Double_dimdimch

Published by Telemachus Press, LLC
http://www.telemachuspress.com

Visit the author website:
http://www.Artpmeister.com

ISBN: 978-1-942899-81-5 (eBook)
ISBN: 978-1-942899-82-2 (Paperback)

Version 2016.08.25

10 9 8 7 6 5 4 3 2 1

What People Are Saying:

Art Meister has written a unique and important introduction every first line supervisor should know about managing others in today's changing times, and what all ranking officers should be aware as well. He deals with sensitive and rarely discussed issues that impact every level of law enforcement with a practical and common sense approach. Art helps set a solid foundation for law enforcement supervisors to better manage the modern workplace.

Dr. Henry C. Lee
Commissioner (Ret), Connecticut State Police
Founder, Henry Lee Institute of Forensic Science
Distinguished Chair Professor, University of New Haven

Considering the events of the last two years, essential management skills have seldom been more critical to a profession that seems under attack. Too often we expect leadership magic from people in managerial and executive positions. However, those same people may have never mastered the basic decision-making skills and ethical frameworks that form true leaders. This book provides important insights into the building blocks that form strong, ethical, trusted organizations. This is essential reading for new managers.

Ronald T. Hosko, President, Law Enforcement Legal Defense Fund, Alexandria, Va., and former Assistant Director (Ret.) Criminal Investigative Division, Federal Bureau of Investigation.

This book is ideal for new first line supervisors. Additionally, I strongly recommend it for anyone approaching the point in their career that makes them eligible for promotion. It gives a great description of what will be expected of them should they advance.

Bernard R. Sullivan, Chief of Police (Ret.), city of Hartford, Connecticut, Commissioner (Ret.), Connecticut State Police and Public Safety, and Vice-Chair of the Sandy Hook Commission to review the Newtown, Connecticut, elementary school shootings.

Art Meister has authored a book on police supervision that should be required reading by every recently promoted supervisor. I wish there had been such an informative guide available when I was first promoted and responsible for personnel, some who were older and had more longevity in law enforcement. Meister outlines a number of pitfalls that could ensnare the unsuspecting supervisor and cause serious, if not fatal damage to his or her career. The examples and information in this book are applicable not just for municipal agencies, but all levels of government supervision in law enforcement.

Joseph P. Faughnan, The Federal U.S. Marshal for the District of Connecticut, former Chief of Police (Ret.) town of Clinton, Connecticut, and Major (Ret.), Connecticut State Police.

Art Meister has captured the important lessons that every first line supervisor in public safety should be taught. I only wish he had written it sooner. I would have benefitted greatly from a book like this. It is a must-read for all new supervisors in our business.

James H. Davis, Special Agent in Charge, (Ret.) Denver Division, Federal Bureau of Investigation. Executive Director (Ret.), Colorado Department of Public Safety. Homeland Security Advisor to former Colorado Governor John Hickenlooper. Board of Directors for the Mizel Institute, and the Denver Police Foundation.

DEDICATION

To Lois, Mildred, and Cathy-Jo

Acknowledgements

There are many people to thank for this book. The unnamed legions of those who served as examples for what works and what doesn't in the world of management.

However, there were those who agreed to read and provide guidance for this book as it developed, and to whom I am deeply indebted. Mr. Richard Ayres, J.D., retired FBI Chief of the FBI Academy's Management Science Unit, co-author of the book, "Leading to Make a Difference," and currently an independent consultant on management issues. Paul Gardner, retired FBI and current Chief of Police for the Georgetown, South Carolina Police Department. Mr. Oliver Halle, J.D., LLM., Retired FBI, author of a book, "Taking the Harder Right," who runs a consulting business based on the book for the public and private sectors. Daniel Halter, retired FBI, and former Supervisor in the FBI's National Center for the Analysis of Violent Crime. John Solomon, former State Trooper, State's Attorney Investigator, and retired Chief of Police for the Easton, Connecticut, Police Department. Joseph Wolfinger, Retired Assistant Director, FBI, co-author of the book, "Rico," who helped me navigate the initial steps to publication. To all I extend sincere gratitude and best wishes.

Also, special thanks for the late Robert Geoghan, retired State Police Sergeant and successful business executive, for setting such a great example of what inspirational supervision should be. To the late Hillary Robinette, retired FBI, author of a seminal book, "Burnout in Blue," who graciously mentored me in the art of program development and instruction for managing marginal and unsatisfactory performance.

I also wish to thank my editor, Karen Lieberman, PhD, who helped make this a readable and instructive product. To Johnny Breeze for designing the cover from a general idea, and MaryAnn Nocco for her help in patiently facilitating this book's completion, and to everyone at Telemachus I extend my heartfelt appreciation.

I must also thank my wife, Sandra, for putting up with the long hours on the computer and the highs and lows of its progress. My daughter, Sarah, continues to be an inspiration for my endeavors, and I appreciate both she and her husband, Phil Coco, for helping with the cyber challenges encountered along the way.

Table of Contents

The Bottom Line

A Management Primer for First Line
Law Enforcement Supervisors

Introduction

Today's technology is rapidly changing how law enforcers interact with the public, especially with regard to interpersonal approaches and actions. Viral video and social media has law enforcement policies and practices directly in the crosshairs of controversy. Behind this phenomenon lies every agency's management role and culpability. That is why the first line supervisor—the manager closest to the actual delivery of services—is so important to law enforcement's future in this new age.

The first line supervisor (Corporal, Sergeant, Supervisory Special Agent and Deputy, etc) has always been the most important position in law enforcement's management hierarchy. *It's where the rubber meets the road for ensuring a mission gets done as expected.* And yet, it is the position least likely to receive any kind of management training when and where it is needed most—at the outset of one's venture into managing others.

This book was written to address this void, to provide newly promoted law enforcement supervisors a basic understanding of the complex role he or she must fill sooner rather than later. It also addresses the importance of knowing their bottom line with regard to handling controversy and conflict, and how best to keep the workplace professional while dealing with challenges unique to this profession.

With that said, to each new supervisor:

Now it's your turn.

Up until now, you've sat in roll call or a group meeting looking at the podium. You've stood before the supervisor's desk asking a question, being critiqued or requesting permission. Now, it's *you* behind the desk or the podium, in a position that is still near, but yet apart from those with whom you've formerly worked as an equal. And it's not just the view that is different. Changing how you will think and act in this new role will pose your biggest challenge. Although most of your knowledge and beliefs remain the same, what will matter is how they'll coalesce into the broader demands and requirements of your supervisory position for effectively interacting with your subordinates. That will define your success or failure in the new role you must fill.

What you did before was fairly straightforward and somewhat easier; you had responsibility only for your own behavior and productivity. Now, you're responsible for the actions and work of those under your supervision. It involves the new dimension of a role. Role, you say? What is that? Well, it's not what you did before. This book will explain how.

This book began as a larger endeavor aimed at how best to deal with problem employees. However, it soon became apparent how critical good management orientation is in dealing with problem employee issues—and how great the need is for those in management to properly understand what management *should* be. New supervisors need to know their proper roles *before* the demands of daily duties occupy their time and attention. This perspective became the driving factor for this book.

I have three primary goals for this book:

*Give the newly promoted a basic understanding of the proper role he or she must fulfill as a supervisor/manager.

*Have the reader revisit their understanding of honesty, loyalty, and friendship to better prepare them for conflict driven decision making.

*Provide the first line supervisor with knowledge that will enhance his or her coaching and counseling skills.

**

To accomplish this, the book is divided into three sections. The first describes how to get a good grasp of your role. Understanding your role helps set the right tenor for your management style and creates a solid bottom line approach for dealing with problem employee issues.

Most managers are promoted to first line supervisory positions without the benefit of any formal management training. They are immediately confronted by functional responsibilities and have little time to think about themselves, or to ponder how they can best adapt to this new set of circumstances, obligations, and responsibilities. Too often they end up doing what they perceive others expect of them without the benefit of learning what they themselves should know to properly fulfill the true nature of their new position.

The second section discusses the manager's bottom line when confronted by challenges that can pit honesty against the strong bonds of loyalty and friendship. It is important to have a good understanding of what friendship and loyalty are when faced with a dilemma that puts either in opposition to one's sworn role. Having a good grasp of this concept *NOW* can help prevent future mistakes when faced with demands from employees or situations that can occur in volatile, controversial and time sensitive situations.

The third section deals with how best to handle the kinds of problems that arise even in the most professionally run workplaces, like over-reactions, sex related matters, social media, whistle blowers, informants, etc.

Much of the material in this book can apply to every level of rank and position, from patrol or investigation to chief or director. However, it is primarily written for those who need it most—the newly promoted supervisors with little or no formal management training. It is designed to enhance counseling and coaching skills, which can be passed on to those in need of professional knowledge, experience, and an appropriate management perspective. The findings and assertions in this book are based on personal experiences, training classes, surveys, and seminars conducted throughout my law enforcement career, and in retirement as a consultant on managing problem employees and workplace violence matters.

The opinions and information contained in this book do not represent any official position of the Federal Bureau of Investigation.

Author's note

He was different, that's for sure. He would be the first of only a couple of other truly inspirational leaders I ever worked for.

Due to a political restructuring, this detective sergeant was reassigned to supervise a patrol platoon in what many would consider to be a demotion, a step back in one's career. But not him. With no indication of regret or disappointment, he assumed his new duties with surprising determination and genuine enthusiasm.

He was a tough guy with a gruff exterior, who could cut to the quick on issues where he sensed unnecessary distraction or ambivalence. He demanded little, but expected a lot. He addressed <u>every</u> operational issue with the same verve and tenacity as if it were a major case, (which meant he could be a pain in the neck sometimes, too). His approach was based on a principle he often espoused, "If you don't work the little cases well, you won't be ready when the Big One comes along."

Yet, he took the time to teach and pitched in to help where needed. He was open to ideas and input and had a great sense of humor. He seemed genuinely interested in and respectful of his subordinates and aggressively supported them against unwarranted criticism, bureaucratic obstacles, or improper outside influences.

What I noticed then, but didn't appreciate until later, was the positive effect his unique ability to inspire had on a couple of less than adequate performers under his purview. As everyone else bought into his leadership persona, they became less tolerant and more critical of the inadequate employees' shenanigans. Those employees soon fell in line, too, and became less problematic. This supervisor had a special something that others did not, a kind of force of personality that commanded immediate respect and attention wherever he went.

I've encountered a couple of other examples of that special something that should be noted, too. A newly appointed Special Agent in Charge swept into command with the same kind of impact that transformed everything in a quick and significantly positive way. Although less gruff and direct than the previous example, he was equally capable of stimulating and motivating everyone in his command. A third example involved the head of an instructional unit who was more modest, low key, yet equally appealing.

Each of these examples had differing personalities, but they had common qualities that propelled them above the many other managers who did their job well, but who lacked that special something that would have made them more effective—even great. I have spent my career exploring what that unique quality is that made each of these examples stand apart from their peers, and my findings are the center of this book. I believe the special something not only powers the heart of management potential, but can have positive side benefits for impacting mediocre and/or problem employee performance, as well.

The Special Something

What did these very different examples share, which seemed to transcend the norm for management capabilities in the workplace?

I found that much revolved around the force of their personalities. By *force* I mean an orientation toward engaging others in <u>a deeply committed, proactive, yet humanely responsive manner</u>. One was tough and direct, the second open and engaging, and the third more demure—three different styles, yet similar management orientations, which reflected what they valued most.

What was so special?

These leaders lived by principles and values that propelled them <u>beyond ego and self aggrandizement.</u> Each possessed a persuasive potency, which earned greater allegiance and sincere effort from subordinates. They were wholly committed to mission and got everyone to buy in, too. *It was like they were on a journey to someplace special and you were invited to come along.* These leaders were confident in not just knowing what had to be done, but how everything *should* and *could* be done.

These select few held principles as their guiding lights, which anchored their outlook in spite of all the noise that went on around them. Their deeply committed beliefs shaped their orientation and ultimately their exceptional personae.

Furthermore, they appeared to hold themselves accountable to personal standards that often exceeded those of the organizations in which they worked. Additionally, they were genuinely interested in and respectful of subordinate needs and welfare, and seemed to value my presence as much as I did theirs. Even when they offered criticism, I felt it was deserved and was with genuine concern and a desire to correct and improve. I often found myself accepting it without being defensive, knowing it was well meant and not punitive or denigrating in any way. When any of these leaders walked into the room, I never felt fear or regret, nor did I ignore their presence. I valued their presence and was truly glad to see them. I feared most the prospect of not meeting their expectations because I didn't want to let them down. They *earned* my allegiance and fealty. They didn't just manage my workday—they took me to a new level of experience.

Those were the common features of their very different personalities that combined to create the something they had that most others did not. It generated the amount of respect and confidence everyone had in their abilities, and showed why subordinates highly valued their association with them. This book is designed to explore the principles, values, expectations, and beliefs that help define that critical extra something of which all newly promoted, first line managers should be aware. It will help you to better navigate the volatile realm of human interaction **and** make you more effective in dealing with problems encountered along the way.

PART I

The Importance of Understanding your Role

The best defense against any management problem is having a good offense. A good offense means being aware of and using the best management practices available and doing so in a timely manner. Too often, an employee problem is the symptom of a performance issue that has been allowed to fester. However, it's not just a matter of knowing the best practices; it also includes knowing how they should be employed. And there lies the essence of the supervisory role.

Regardless of the work environment/culture—from austere to open—the extent of any leader's influence is sustainable only to the point others are willing to let it affect them. Power and authority can be fleeting. Mutiny is not a word normally associated with organizational theory, but it happens. From surreptitiously undermining output to open rebellion, it dwells at the core of your potential to affect others and how others can affect you. A problem employee's escapade that becomes public indirectly taints management's reputation as well. The inevitable question gets asked: "Where had management been before this became an issue?" A role properly fulfilled not only helps lessen the potential for personnel problems, reprisal and/or workplace violence—it will strengthen any official action needed to address a problem employee.

How many newly promoted managers get the opportunity to explore their relationship with the position they will occupy <u>before</u> the onslaught of responsibilities takes command of their time and attention? Too often employees are promoted into first line management positions without the training and opportunity to really think and learn about the new role they must fill. They are seldom prepared for this transition in a manner that helps them understand *role* sooner rather than later. Many bring former interpersonal habits and reasoning power into a new position. One day you're sitting in a patrol car, cubicle or bull pen, and the next behind the podium, in an enclosed office, or at the wheel of a supervisor's car amidst a swirl of new responsibility and expectation. Standard Operating Procedures (SOPs) often become the dominant—sometimes singular—focus of a new manager's attention.

But there's more to management than just knowing the book cover to cover. Knowing and properly fulfilling your management *role* will not only enhance your ability to influence others, but help reduce the likelihood of employee problems. It will better serve both you and the organization during whatever corrective or disciplinary actions are necessary, including any subsequent reviews or adjudication. It's not about the *type* of discipline to be meted out, but <u>how</u> it gets accomplished that gives management the edge for greater success.

CHAPTER 1

The Supervisor's Role

Whatever your view in the debate over what differentiates a manager and a leader, understanding your role applies to both, and could determine the difference between being great versus good, unique over normal, and influential as opposed to ineffectual.

When actors audition for a part in a play, they read or recite lines from a script. A director will assess the actor's overall delivery to determine how he/she fits the characteristics and nuances of the role that character will play in the entire production. The actor's preparation and delivery should include an understanding of that role, so the appropriate mannerisms, voice, and theatrics are employed to get the part. In other words, there's a lot more to a part than simply knowing and reciting lines.

The same can be applied to the role of a management position, except that your script is usually a manual of rules, regulations, and standard operating procedures. How well you know or quote them won't guarantee your success. They are only the script for a part you must play to fulfill a role in a much larger production. *This is not to imply that managing is acting, but in some ways it requires a similar skill set—and for some more so than others.*

That's because there's more to managing than just fulfilling fundamental job responsibilities, i.e., planning, organizing, directing, staffing, coordinating, reporting, and budgeting (PODSCORB) and variations thereof. It requires the ability to see beyond the realm of immediate responsibility with vision and greater comprehension of what it is managers should also do—<u>recognize and accept</u> that subordinates have reasonable expectations of management, too. Law enforcement managers must *also believe* in the importance of their position and the public's trust, *while managing* change and achieving maximum productivity for a common purpose through <u>others (subordinates)</u>. Whew! There is a lot to a management role.

The Persona of a First Line Management Position

"Rank has its privileges" is an old saying, which implies that those in higher positions enjoy a favored standing, i.e., preference and priority. Therefore they may be less obligated to observe certain basic social courtesies: *They* didn't have to stand in line, *they* got first choice, and *they* were less accountable for mistakes, etc. In other words, privilege, accommodation, and value can gravitate to the newly promoted leaving everyone else behind. Rank then seems designed to serve the individual more than the individual serves the rank.

Not Anymore!

Today's management world is vastly different. For one thing, it's much more sensitized. Major historical Civil Rights, labor, and crime control legislation has re-engineered management practices to a modern model of greater employee accommodation and caution. Rank or position doesn't automatically bestow anything to the newly promoted—sometimes not even higher pay in cases where overtime is no longer included. Rank has evolved its own persona in the form of bottom line and very reasonable subordinate expectations. Every supervisor must recognize, accept, and adjust to, these expectations in order to be effective in today's management realm

The word *persona* is used to embody inherent principles and values that most subordinates expect from *every* management position <u>and</u> from the person promoted into it. One could consider these expectations the real DNA of good management for every position within the chain of command. Walk by a recently vacated supervisor's office that is awaiting a replacement. The position still exists. Think about what you might expect from whoever will occupy it. How will that person measure up to what you expect is appropriate for that position? It is amazing how influential just the office or rank can be to subordinates—even those with greater competence and knowledge than whoever occupies it. So, the question becomes, will the persona of the newly promoted manager be a good fit with what is expected of the position to be occupied?

If you were asked to sum up the content of the typical management training program with all its myriad theories and practical exercises, you would probably make a simple, yet profound, observation. You would see that most of the knowledge imparted was basically a re-packaging of what your mother taught you growing up: Treat others as you would have them treat you, share and share alike, respect and be civil to one another, never interrupt, always excuse yourself, say thank you, and don't make fun of others. She probably also included owning up to your mistakes and doing the right thing. These simple little rules of decency and humanity are important to any kind of human endeavor. For every management position, there *is* a core foundation of simple human principles and values that most subordinates expect from whoever occupies the position. These principles and values will comprise the persona of the position and should become the underpinning of however you choose to manage or lead. They are what most subordinates will expect at the very least.

Principles versus Values

Principles are fundamental truths, laws, doctrine or assumptions that guide our daily actions as part of our cultural heritage and social order (*respect for others and the law, being honest and fair, etc.*). They grow out of religious, philosophical, family and community-wide acceptance of their legitimacy and importance (ex: *Golden Rules*). These principles also play a role in what we choose to value. Within the chaos of multiple tasks and challenges, principles are the guiding lights to which one will want to stay true—regardless of the challenge being faced.

Values, on the other hand, are preferences. We *choose* to value certain things over others. They're mostly personal and subjective. They are matters of relative worth—something one would intrinsically desire more than something else (for ex: friends, to whom or what to be loyal, wealth, adventure, risk, etc.). Those we prefer play a large part in making us different individually and influence how we relate to and interact with everything.

Principles help us sense what is right, while the values we choose can either help us head in the right direction or lead us astray.

Next, let's look at subordinate *expectations* of the position you now occupy, which are comprised of principles and values that should underlie your role as a manager.

CHAPTER 2

Bottom Line Subordinate Expectations

Every organization has management goals, objectives, rules, regulations, and operating procedures that lay out what is expected of employees. But, employees have expectations of management, too. When surveyed about what they needed most from management, police supervisors *and* officers most often listed the following expectations (however *you* choose to consider them, either principles or values). Despite advances in technology and the way people interact with one another, bottom line employee expectations have remained consistent. Two expectations—respect and civility—stood out among the rest. These serve as the backdrop to all the others.

<u>**Respect**</u>: plays a huge role in everyone's life—even those undeserving of it.

(It has been both my experience and observation that the most productive informants, those that deliver the best information over extended periods of time, are those that are treated with at least the dignity of civil discourse and honest proffer, regardless of how despicable one may be).

From infancy to old age, from inner city playgrounds to the highest office in the land, respect is a baseline component of each individual's sense of wellbeing and ego. It is the essential component of how we value ourselves. In general, most feel and extend respect through socially preferred expressions of deference, civility, manners, courtesy, proper exercise of authority, etc. Yes, there are those who distort this value by associating it more with fear and subjugation, but most recognize that **to get it one must give it**.

Regardless of how you may feel personally, as a manager there are considerations that have a cause beyond your own emotions or inclinations. *It's not about massaging egos or feeling a sense of hypocrisy to show respect when you may feel the employee doesn't deserve it.* The mission or service to be delivered may require tempering personal feelings for a more appropriate outcome. <u>Respect must be afforded a subordinate in every interaction,</u> at least to the extent that it conveys the benefit of any doubt, which includes proper deference and control of emotion that is free of any denigration, humiliation, and/or exploitation. When credit is due, give it willingly despite the employee's previous behavior or reputation. Any kind of folly at the expense of the employee should be avoided without exception.

<u>Civility</u>: Has to do with how respect is communicated—particularly in times of stress or confrontation. A manager may feel an employee does not deserve respect, but it (respect) should be *the* standard for getting every message across—*especially* when the issue is controversial or confrontational. Anything less moves a conflict out of the professional realm into the emotional arena, and it can undermine your effectiveness. In addition, it could weaken a manager's position in relation to later reviews or adjudication of problem employee issues.

It is unrealistic to think there are no exasperating employees and/or consternating situations, or that raising one's voice, expressing frustration, or being short on occasion doesn't happen. The key, however, is the manner in which you do it, especially one's choice of wording.

Unfortunately, there exist roughshod and demeaning management personalities that achieve successful results. There are a few notable coaches, CEOs, and others who push and pummel people into a winning season or two through fear, intimidation, and humiliation. Because of their overbearing antics, they seem to attract the most publicity and undeserved credibility. They make the work experience one of survival for so many. However, most of these ill-tempered personalities soon move on to other challenges—leaving in their wake a notable, but basically short-term, dysfunctional success for someone else to clean up. Fortunately, there are more managers that achieve longer term results by managing more in line with the principles and values of the characteristics described above.

The National Football League provides a visible example of this kind of dichotomy. There are coaches who curse, slap helmets, and publicly admonish and humiliate players, yet take their team to a winning season or two. But the coaches and owners who eschew those antics and choose to manage in a more deliberate, reasoned, and professional manner (Joe Gibbs, Washington Redskins; Tony Dungy, Indianapolis Colts; Bill Belichick, New England Patriots), grow their teams beyond the winning season and become a dynasty. (Hall of Fame Coach Don Shula was volatile early in his NFL career and blew up at players. Shula says he learned over time that restraining his anger made him more effective.) [1]

That's not to say a well placed expletive or shout isn't warranted on occasion, but when that kind of bloviating and abuse begins to dominate one's personality, *it could* mean the difference between an occasional, but unlikely, winning season versus a longer term dynasty.

You can raise your voice and still be civil. One can be tough and professional without the disrespectful transgressions that frustrations can induce, such as emotional outbursts, tirades of expletives, and

---

1 James Lavin, *Management Secrets of the New England Patriots,* Vol. 2, (Stamford, Ct. Pointer Press 2005), 327.

abusive behavior. Having the self restraint to say (with emphasis) "I'm *very* disappointed" or "I'm finding it hard to understand your position" is always better than shouting "You idiot!" Or, "How can you be so stupid!" *The very nature of promotion carries the expectation of judicious behavior and assessment. Accepting this reality is an important part of fulfilling a management role.*

It stands to reason that subordinates who truly admire, respect, and trust their leader will do more to the best of their abilities—even those assignments they may not like doing (*someone has to attend the autopsy or guard the garage*).

Performance critiques and corrections are more effective when accomplished without the denigration of insulting language or public humiliation. Critiques and corrections should always be done away from peers in a civil and constructive manner—even though you may not like the person or feel they are deserving of this accommodation.

Other Expectations

There are many and varied principles and values that could be applied to a management role, but respect and civility will set the tone and tenor throughout them all. The following principles and values are those most frequently mentioned as subordinate expectations and serve as the foundation for an effective management role:

Competency: Naturally whoever occupies the position should possess the qualifications and probity to hold it in order to provide the necessary knowledge, experience and support, which will help subordinates do their job the *right* way. Also, subordinates expect a promotion to be based on merit and established procedure and not for another (political) reason. It is also important for the newly promoted to know and be willing to admit the limits of his or her knowledge. *No one admires anyone who thinks they know more than everyone else and interacts accordingly.* Knowing SOPs is easy. Executing them effectively will be the challenge. **Always strive to improve by helping those with less knowledge and experience while listening to those with more.**

Vision

Competence is a lot more than just knowing. *Seeing* is probably the most important element of overall competence for a law enforcement manager. The ability to visualize and prognosticate likely outcomes from questionable circumstances is a very important quality. One who can visualize actions that, by themselves, indicate no wrongdoing, but which combine with other subtleties to raise a specter of unethical, illegal, or unreasonable behavior will be a more effective manager. However, it also means being cognizant of the "aura" of your position. It could unintentionally legitimize, or seemingly sanction something that may seem innocuous or slightly shady, but your knowledge or participation risks greater consequence. *Officers decide to hold a retirement party at a local strip joint and invite you, the supervisor, to attend. Officers get a special deal with a local disreputable business, and you wish to save a few bucks, too. An employee who is emceeing an office luncheon in a public venue gets carried away with inappropriate language or topics.* Interacting with subordinates in a supportive and social way while protecting the department's valid interests on a more astute and conceptual level can be a difficult line to straddle.

As a manager you add another dimension, one with greater consequences, to a problem should something occur that becomes public knowledge, either with or without your participation. But that is what management competency requires—the ability to see the gravity of circumstances (refer to addendum) that others may not.

Immediately attend to any hint of wrongdoing (racial profiling, sexual harassment, any kind of unprofessional act). Pay attention to negative implications of language or innuendo in reports, emails, or letters. Always maintain a good sense of proper protocol and professionalism. Also, be careful with what <u>you</u> say, as it will become a history of <u>your</u> actions—words and deeds recorded or remembered that may haunt you later on.

True professionals have a keen sense of ramification in real time, and conduct themselves accordingly. Therefore, the best way to avoid future problems is to act professionally <u>now</u> and do what a proper role requires—regardless of culture or environment. Besides, subordinates look to management for example, direction, and support, <u>not</u> friendship, camaraderie, or entertainment.

Fairness: must apply to both access and application in equal measure (in being accessible to all, allocating assignments, conducting performance evaluation, and discipline)—even to those one may not like. Being fair is the glue that holds an organization together. Being accessible is not just sitting in an office with the door open. Whoever occupies a management position has to <u>make it happen</u>. This means actively engaging, and especially LISTENING, to <u>all</u> components. One must allocate time proportionately, avoiding over focus on favorites at the expense of others. Subordinates expect that whoever occupies a managerial position will steer clear of extremes and compromise where necessary. It is important to ensure all subordinate assessments are based on actual performance and not personal bias or unrealistic or petty expectations (*over emphasizing shined shoes and clean cars versus team work and solid results*). In addition, everyone, including superstars, must be held equally accountable for established performance standards and requirements.

Whether you like them or not, the New England Patriots football team is noted as much for their strong organizational prowess as they are for their winning *seasons. Current and former Patriot players often talk about the "Patriot Way," how management treats all the players the same from the rookie to the super stars, and how <u>everyone</u> in the organization is goal-oriented, sacrificing short term gains and personal agendas for longer term consistency. The team is very successful at turning relative unknowns and, in some cases, publicity seeking malcontents or ego driven personalities into team players.[2]*

Trust: Trust in the workplace is the oil for relationships and organizational cohesion. It has a lot to do with transparency, consistency, and honesty. It is an important part of one's ability to form relationships. Trust implies a sense of reciprocity, at least to the extent each can rely on the other to live up to certain expectations. *Leaders rightfully expect loyalty from subordinates, but must also understand subordinates expect loyalty from management, too.* Trust is closely associated with faith. In other words, believing and counting on something unproven or unknown as in future intent or actions.

This expectation is best fulfilled through open communication. Good managers do not hoard information. They freely share proposed policy and work schedule changes, upcoming special assignments, budget issues, promotional or transfer opportunities, a colleague in need of help or a special occasion, and many other ancillary, but important information for subordinates to know.

Institutional trust comes from believing the organization is founded on sound principles and dedicated to doing the right and reasonable thing; and those responsible for its operation consistently espouse and do what's right, as well. The more one knows of another and greater familiarity and consistency one feels in a manager's words and deeds, the more faith he/she will have that he or she will perform as expected. It becomes an intuitive belief based on experience and

2 Ibid., 326

sometimes hearsay. (*A trusted source tells you another can be trusted on the basis of their experience.*)

Whoever occupies the management position must be available and <u>willing</u> to discuss and deal with subordinate concerns with enough transparency to satisfy them about your sincerity. How trusting subordinates are about discussing matters of personal importance will be in direct proportion to the openness of the manager. He or she must deal with issues in a sincere, honest, and informative way without false promises, misleading information, bias, or personal agenda.

Good managers are visible, not to micromanage, but to give direction and help solve subordinate problems. Subordinates want to know you are there to help, not hinder. When closed door sessions with a select few become commonplace, or something promised becomes something else, or established procedure gets reworked for convenience or dupery, then suspicion, disappointment, and a sense of betrayal can rear their ugly heads. Rumors can kill unit cohesion and esprit de corps.

<u>Courage</u>: To *Be* a manager and do what's *Right!* Whoever occupies the position must confront and deal with all issues in a fair, transparent, and timely manner—especially those that take them out of their comfort zone. *We usually know what the right thing to do is, but lack the courage or hesitate too long to do it.* This would include vigorously defending subordinates against unfair charges when they are right, or extending them the benefit of any doubt until issues are resolved. Always hold *everyone* accountable to established standards and levels of performance.

Courage includes having the gumption to make hard decisions based on fair, rational, and transparent reasoning when it involves work assignments, transfers, discipline and other actions within a manager's purview, and to correct, coach, and counsel <u>when necessary</u> and appropriate. It means providing the kind of feedback that helps to train, develop, and maintain one's professional bearing and not just saying what subordinates like to hear or what you think would make you more popular. This could include assigning marginal and problem employees what they are required to do and addressing their performance accordingly, and not relegating them to lesser roles— *thereby failing accountability and further enabling their deficiency.* Most subordinates respect and admire managers who can admit mistakes and take responsibility for their own actions—the kind that may even hurt on occasion, but the right thing to do.

If there is one noteworthy management-related deficiency in problem employee issues, it is 'avoidance' (inadequate or absentee supervision). Most severe problem employee issues begin with tolerating episodes of marginal or unsatisfactory performance that fester and grow from there. That's because any corrective action involves conflict, and there are many who consciously avoid that kind of discomfort out of fear, dread, or inconvenience.

As the former manager of the pennant winning New York Yankees, Joe Torre reflected in his book *Ground Rules for Winners*, when dealing with management issues, "Sometimes you have to feel the fear, and just do it anyway. That's courage!"[3] If it's more of a dread (the disinclination to tackle a difficult situation) than fear, then it may be just a matter of having the motivation and fortitude (gumption) to just *do it.*

When viewing the empty office to be filled by you, most subordinates will expect and hope you will be competent, respectful, and civil. Every worker wants a manager that is fair and trustworthy, and has the courage to back employees up when warranted.

---

3 Joe Torre with Henry Dreher, *Joe Torre's Ground Rules for Winners. (New York, Hyperion. 1999)* 129

These subordinate expectations for management positions can be enhanced and expanded through the *artistry* of whoever occupies the position.

When it comes to artistry, there are innate or developed skills, attributes, and abilities a manager can bring to the position, which can significantly enhance their effectiveness and surpass bottom line subordinate expectations. Foremost is to truly like what you do.

Enthusiasm!

"Enthusiasm can be aroused by two things; first, an ideal which takes the imagination by storm, and second, the definite, intelligible plan for carrying that ideal into practice."

—*British historian Arnold Toynbee*

Mr. Toynbee hits on the true essence of leadership. Enthusiasm is an important part of it. It significantly impacts not only the employee expectations listed herein, but *everything* one does.

Enthusiasm enriches the principles and values comprising subordinate expectations that will be unique to each manager's repertoire of skills and abilities. One example would be taking civility and building upon it with voice inflection, focus, sincerity, and choice of approach and wording, thereby making it more inspiring and dynamic. It's how you apply personality (enthusiasm) and character (principle) to each value that makes it unique to you. It is a key ingredient for bolstering one's capability to make more out of whatever is required. This, in turn, will underlie the *artistry* behind anyone's capacity to make a difference.

Working around people who enjoy what they do makes for a great work experience. Sincere enthusiasm can be contagious. It helps to truly like what you do, even if management's not what you thought it would be. Much of this quality comes from self confidence fed from a strong personal commitment to mission *and* purpose. It reflects the passion that comes from believing in and wanting to do what you do in spite of negative or counterproductive influences around you. It is an asset that must be nurtured continuously and maintained— especially in the face of distressing situations.

Most everyone's initial attraction to law enforcement had some element of idealism—a belief in the goodness and importance of this occupation. Anyone who has worked for a truly enthusiastic boss soon realizes the force that kind of personality can have over others regardless of the culture, environment, or working conditions. Former Army General and U.S. President Dwight D. Eisenhower once said, "*What counts is not necessarily the size of the dog in the fight, but the size of the fight in the dog.*" It pertains to the orientation that comes from within the person occupying a position of power. It helps power the force of enthusiasm. It is something to consider when reflecting on your personal approach for fulfilling a new managerial role.

On the other hand:

Cynicism

Being overly cautious, critical, questioning, or disbelieving is a difficult balancing act for law enforcers. On the one hand, it is a useful perspective to have when dealing with adversarial investigative situations and subjects. However, it can become detrimental to one's personal and professional life. Controlling cynicism is a challenge.

Being overly cynical can be dangerous to one's health. Too much adversity and negativism can erode a balanced attitude. Those overexposed to hostility, confrontation, and trauma must balance their experiences in some way. Not all kids are delinquents, druggies, or truants, and everyone isn't scamming the system. Maybe it's time to get involved in some other more positive areas of human interaction like coaching or teaching. Managers must continually be aware of this dilemma, and do something to help correct it. *Community policing can play an important role in this area of concern. It not only enhances a department's relationship with the community, but just as importantly, it helps the officer counterbalance the effects of cynicism. It requires him or her to purposely and routinely engage law abiding people in a non-enforcement context, those who may at least understand, even truly appreciate what he or she does as a law enforcer.*

For those who've allowed cynicism to infect their persona, it may mean revisiting and revitalizing what originally attracted them to the career that reality has burnished over the years. *Anyone who has witnessed a cadet graduation knows the sheen of each new officer's face, which reflects their sense of accomplishment for completing their training regimen and the anticipation to fulfill what they always wanted to do.* What happens to that sheen as experience and reality pummel their careers?

Keeping One's Career a Calling

Those enforcing the law and keeping the peace develop a set of unique skills and abilities that are different from the general population. The suspicion laden and adversarial nature of police work builds intuitive abilities which enable officers and investigators to address human interactive issues from a different perspective. Based on this skill, law enforcers very often see what others do not and interact accordingly. This ability factors heavily into the fulfillment of a very noble and essential purpose for maintaining social order—the mainframe of our democratic way of life—regardless of what others may not see or think.

It is important to keep in mind that most people get to live the lives they wish because of what law enforcers do for a living. All of this factors into an endeavor that is much more than just a job. There are other dangerous jobs out there, but when one chooses to face and endure emotional and physical risks for the sake of others (public service over self), as is the nature of police work, it places law enforcement work in a higher realm.

Those who are able to withstand the ravages of difficult times and maintain the appeal of ideals that attracted them in the first place, are the ones with greater potential to affect others in a positive way. Managers of law enforcers should regularly espouse this sentiment to subordinates. Believing it yourself helps move your management style closer to inspirational leadership.

Gratitude!

Don't just think you have it. You've got to show it! It is easy to do. It's another way to express appreciation, and employees love to hear it. Just make sure it is sincere. Sincerity of gratitude rises in proportion to the timeliness and artfulness of its application. Don't delay. Do it when it is observed and earned. Any kind of length of service recognition (pin or certificate) shouldn't be left in a mail slot or on a desk. It should be personalized. Yes, the occasional award ceremony and performance evaluation is a good way to show it officially, but it shouldn't preclude you from personally expressing your gratitude directly. Regardless of how tough or competent one is—everyone likes being told they are appreciated for what they do. It could be as simple as saying "You know, Bob, I thought you did a very good job in resolving that issue yesterday." Your voice inflection, eye contact, and personalized attention all go a long way to help the employee feel a measure of their value. When they deserve it, tell the group what they do is important, and how proud you are of their effort. It pays off in all sorts of ways.

Compassion, empathy, sympathy, concern …

These are very important and often underutilized intangibles of your role. Most of the attention paid to subordinates by management revolves around regulation, control, and productivity. While employees are paid to fulfill the needs of the organization, there is human emotion that may not relate to the tasks assigned, but nevertheless accompanies them into the workplace and impacts those responsibilities. Apart from that which requires oversight and direction to achieve required output, there are employee needs, anxieties, problems, and uncertainties that may require attention. And, as the first line supervisor, you become the most apparent face of the organization.

In many work environments there is a huge gap between employee needs and management's awareness of those needs. In many cases there is little the supervisor can do. However, that shouldn't preclude at least some sympathy or concern being expressed or shown by management. Managers who fill this gap with genuine concern, empathy, and compassion help lessen the inevitable distance and discourse that can result between management and first line employees.

Unfortunately, there are too many male dominated environments where a subtle, if not direct undertone of bravado influences employees to think otherwise (Suck it up Fella!). Showing compassion or concern is not handholding, as it is sometimes negatively perceived, but expressing a personal interest in another's life that helps <u>facilitate continued productivity</u> and avoids slumps or increased negativity along the way.

Its one thing to have a human resource department or other resources to help or handle an employee's troubles, but quite another when the personal attention component between manager and employee is likewise delegated away. It should remain part of the equation.

Traumatic circumstances like shootings, serious injuries, and significant loss may have official processes in place to handle the legal, medical, and psychological aspects of a situation, but that shouldn't preclude your continued interest and concern throughout an employee's period of healing. Remain connected, help in any way you can. Talk to the employee. Don't avoid them because of sensitive areas that are uncomfortable. Just listening to someone going through a challenge sends a strong message that management personally cares. Those who can communicate that message stand to help the employee <u>and</u> the organization.

Remember that trauma lingers. Once an individual's issue is disposed of officially (accommodated, counseled, adjudicated), there will still be lingering effects. Someone losing a spouse, or going through a tough divorce, or having experienced a significant emotional event, will most certainly feel the effects months, sometimes years down the road. The loss doesn't stop after a funeral, signing divorce papers, or resolving an internal investigation. Show you care and help whenever you can.

CHAPTER 3

You Have a Position with Great Opportunity

You now have a position that is yours to engage however *you* wish. Will you just occupy the position to manage the status quo, or use the opportunity to take it to another level of competence and output?

Even if the added artistry is lacking, just adhering to the bottom line expectations subordinates have for the position can help prevent problems in the first place. They also bolster a manager's position with whatever dispute resolution processes are in place. Civil service employees have an arsenal of legal weapons to accuse, counter claim, and consternate legitimate efforts to address their performance problems. From claims of discrimination to dereliction of manage-ment duties, there are legal avenues they can use when management strays from the core principles, values, expectations and beliefs of a proper role.

The more managers stay true to core expectations, the less ammo employees have to shoot back at you (both figuratively and some-times literally). What's important to remember is that as the pressure of an escalating controversy intrudes into your time and attention, the challenge will be to adhere to employee bottom line expectations—especially respect and civility. So, the question then becomes—How does your own persona mesh with that of the position you will occupy?

Who You Are, What You Stand For, Matters!

It is an accepted premise that groups eventually take on the persona of the leader. In spite of what the group may expect from the rank or management position, it will be the manager who most influences how subordinates carry out their duties. *An indecisive or overly aggressive manager will see similar traits evolve in subordinate performance.* If that is the case, then how the group does their job lies at the very heart of your measure of success as a manager and that of the overall mission. Your role becomes what you are and how you can adapt to build what is expected from the position you hold. You become the guiding light for how others will fulfill their roles, too.

Each person assuming a management position comes prepackaged with values and principles acquired throughout their lifetime. Their personal character propels an orientation that lies at the heart of how one will view the world and engage in tasks. The manager's persona can seep through or around the persona of the position, and become the dominating influence that determines how subordinate bottom line expectations for the position get reinforced or reworked. Hopefully the new manager's persona is predominantly positive— something one should ponder during times of self reflection. For example, a deep mistrust of people will play itself out in daily interactions like not delegating properly, having a tendency to micro manage, being less open or accessible, or even perceived as contemptuous.

If you were to ask anyone to recall a great boss they invariably mention that he or she was competent, enthusiastic, fair, accessible, caring, etc.,—the interpersonal intangibles that made them particularly effective. Like the actor seeking to play a part, how well you understand and can adapt to the core principles and values expected of the position you occupy will determine how your role will play in the production. *And the Oscar goes to ... Those who are not like the role, yet overcome those differences to make it look like they really fit the role ...*

The Dilemma!

It can easily become a conflict between what *you* want and expect, and what subordinates expect of the management position you now occupy. You may have little patience for others, or possess unrealistic expectations. *Those who believe people must be pushed into action, that they work best when insecure or on edge versus a belief that people are basically good and want to work. These are two opposing orientations, the latter of which meshes best with the persona of the position.* You'll want to ensure that any conflict between your persona and that of the position is not contributing to a problem employee issue. For example, a fear of conflict may further enable a problem employee in the making or, being overly aggressive or expecting too much can push others into rebellion.

The Manager's Persona

During our formative years we are always observing other management roles—from parents, teachers, coaches, and clergy to media moguls, celebrities, and politicians. We tend to adopt aspects of those we think (choosing what to value) achieve effective outcomes according to our sense of values and orientation at the time. One may believe the louder manager who leads by fear gets better results in the short term versus the low key, methodical, deliberate, and more inclusive boss down the hall. While role models come and go, the essence of what management should be (its role) often gets lost in the antics of the more dominant or loudest personality.

The point is that we can too often model the actions of others without first understanding what management <u>should be</u>—how the <u>role</u> it plays in successful outcomes should serve as the true compass for everyone's orientation and behavior. Some get it better than others. One may value a strong work ethic, but a narrow focus on 18-hour days as the best way to show it may be unreasonable for the group. Another may have little patience for whiners and slackers, but dealing with them with disdain and impatience will not achieve a more effective outcome, which a proper role model will do.

So, the question should be: How will <u>your orientation</u> fit the persona (what most subordinates expect) of the position you will occupy in management?

While most enter management with their principles and basic values aligned with those expected of the position, some may require the learning of new traits or behaviors, even adjusting one's basic view of the world to create a better fit. In other words, enhance your abilities by assimilating subordinate expectations for the position into your basic style and demeanor. Not everyone is wound the same in terms of management style, but those closest to the basic principles and values of their proper role get better results over the longer term.

Granted, there are some *variations* with regard to how a role gets fulfilled in certain situations. For example, the role of a more sedate or routine support component within your organization may require a less rigorous approach as opposed to an intensely regimented, specialized unit. *It is difficult to imagine a soft spoken, reserved, and overly cautious persona effectively managing a fast paced, intense, and specialized operation—or a reverse scenario.*

However, in spite of how each role may vary in emphasis or intensity—they both should accommodate subordinate expectations from the same perspective. *A training instructor in a paramilitary environment who refers to recruits as "mister" or "trainee" or other non-demeaning titles, and manages them accordingly, can achieve the same if not better kind of deconstructed mindset for team building as the caustic, and demeaning style of someone else.* A role properly fulfilled goes a long way in protecting the manager <u>and</u> the organization from whatever fallout a problem issue produces during post incident analysis, mediation, and adjudication.

Tough bosses abound, but the one's most respected and effective will be those with the command of presence and restraint, who express that toughness through the principles and values listed herein. They treat everyone the same—from the Chief to the Janitor. They get the point across without the superfluity of demeaning, vulgar, or self-serving actions. It stands to reason one would want to do their best for a respected leader, as opposed to just trying to survive the others.

The point being, one can still be tough <u>and</u> civil, still call the hard shots while feeling empathy and showing sympathy, and still deal effectively with adversity with tact and diplomacy. Those who can restrain from excess, who face consequences straight on, who, under pressure of conflict and crisis, stay true to the values herein are the toughest of all. Intimidation is easy. Controlling emotion is difficult.

One Must Ask Him or Herself

Am I doing what a proper role requires, or just what feeds my own personal wants and ego? What is my management orientation? Is my view of the position I am about to occupy realistic? Do I agree with and can I adapt to the core expectations? What must I change to do so—to create a better fit and make it more effective? That may depend on what <u>you</u> hold as core principles and values.

Acclimating Yourself to Management's Role

Enforcing the law may be just a job to some, but when one assumes the mantle of manager—an aura of 'role' should draw him or her beyond just working at a job. One of the first steps in acquiring a good fit is realizing that management is not a continuation of what you've done before. It will be a new learning experience. Each level of management requires a broadening of skills and abilities. Each will challenge the extent to which you are open to new ideas and information, and how you adapt to the role expected of the position you occupy. It will require adding some additional perspectives to your thinking, which must not just be accommodated, but truly <u>believed</u>.

CHAPTER 4

Basic Beliefs

To start, it is important to understand that leadership can be a somewhat lonely endeavor. The more committed you are to fulfilling its proper role, the more a discernible distance will evolve between you and your former work relationships. A proper management role takes you to a different position in the social order, one which has responsibility for directing and evaluating others. *It's like moving closer to the sun (to the principles and values that drive the organization as a whole versus individual needs and desires).* Your concerns and focus take on a different hue for both yourself and others. It is the reality of a newly promoted supervisor's lot—they (subordinates) are in the bull pen or out doing their job—you're in the office, or riding around ensuring the job is getting done. This line intrudes itself between what was and what is. You may still be invited to parties and other social functions, but your previous level of intimacy and interaction has changed. For any first time manager it can be a sobering experience—caught between the role of your new position and the allegiance of now-subordinate relationships.

To help bolster your role, there are certain beliefs that should be accepted and added to your own management orientation. To believe is to be certain something is true. The following are essential beliefs that help frame a good management orientation.

Belief #1: A noble Calling

Management is a very important part of our social, political, and business fabric. It should be something every manager believes—deeply. Good management gives a group meaning and direction that gets results. When done right it is the catalyst for group progress and survival; when wrong it becomes an obstacle to growth and productivity. It is an essential part of every group dynamic.

No one is dragged kicking and screaming into management roles. It will be the conscious choice of most to take that step. And yet, there are managers who feel self conscious or even a little guilty about their position—especially those who are promoted from within the same unit or group. Some newly promoted managers approach demands and discipline with a sense of insecurity because they are unsure of their role, their comfort zone still entrenched in their prior position and former relationships. Also, there are some who distrust or even disliked management, but took the plunge anyway for more money, power, or prestige. This sense of unease or distrust can manifest itself in many negative ways—from a propensity to express derogatory inferences about management as a way of placating or sustaining former relationships, to thinking subordinates are there *only* to do their (supervisor's) bidding. Both extremes fail to factor in their proper role.

The reality is—the higher one rises in the organization the more they will be judged and related to in different ways by _all_ their former relationships. It becomes another step in personal growth. Your concern and care for your former friends and peers must now be shared equally with others. What you used to do is now one part of another whole, and you're in charge. **So, believe it!** Decide to <u>BE</u> a manager. That means to do what the role requires—<u>all of it</u>. Management truly is an important and worthwhile venture.

Belief #2: A Common Purpose

Regardless of rank or position, every employee's value to the organization has <u>everything</u> to do with how the quality of services and products get <u>delivered</u>. This constitutes the organization's purpose— or why it exists at all. Having a clearly defined mission is a <u>crucial</u> part of this process. _Everyone_ should be attuned to how their efforts impact the delivery of services or products to the customer or user. It is an orientation that helps employees see beyond their immediate circumstances, and gives them a feeling of being part of something larger than their own self-interest. It should be part of everyone's orientation and repertoire, from the Chief down to part-time employees, and conveyed regularly by management in both words <u>and</u> deeds.

Many in support positions consider their customer the internal entity they are directly interacting with, i.e., secretary to boss, dispatcher to patrol. While that may be true in fact—they must be made aware of the stake each has in the larger production—looking beyond their immediate concerns to a clear connection with the organization's mission. For example, try soliciting <u>everyone's</u> input for substantive matters on occasion. You'd be surprised with what many otherwise-neglected employees have to offer. Also, show how delay, denial, or abrasive delivery of a support function can have a negative impact on the quality of service ultimately delivered. _A secretary is deeply committed to you, but holds others in contempt. It may work for you, but can create havoc for those actually delivering service. A desk officer smarting over a recent humiliating interaction with a superior barks back at a caller or a walk-in. An officer frustrated with a difficult personality in payroll takes his or her frustration out on_ *peers or the public. There are examples of employees denied expense re-imbursement without adequate explanation and who then felt compelled to recom-pense through other means, i.e., inflating other expenses, etc.* Both parties to an internal disagreement must consider how their support of a common purpose should include ways to help remedy a negative interaction. One inept or abrasive secretary, dispatcher, or misguided employee can have a profoundly negative impact on another's ability to perform. *Patrol officers do not like hearing sarcasm or surliness from dispatchers or watch commanders over the radio. This kind of negativity can work its way into the interaction between the offended officer and the public where "purpose" gets delivered.*

Therefore, it is important that <u>every</u> employee be aware of that pur-pose and *believes in it.* While it may be difficult to achieve this kind of symmetry in a world of external and internal challenges, such as diffi-cult union negotiations, threats of lay-offs, a dysfunctional hierarchy, adverse publicity, and disciplinary issues, it will be the artistry of the manager that gets everyone beyond whatever problems complicate the issue(s).

You become the moderator/referee between your subordinates and all kinds of internal and external conflict for the good of a preferred outcome—continued equilibrium, production, and delivery of serv-ice. It is the place where the manager's commitment to and imple-mentation of "role" is needed most. This doesn't mean you have to give in or be overly nice to everyone. It's impossible to please every-one all the time. But, it's important to remember "purpose" when dealing with a challenging issue.

How you relate to all employees—even difficult ones—lies at the core of your success in fulfilling your role. *Anyone on the receiving end of a corrective or disciplinary action may not appreciate your effort, but you can bet peers are watching.* It is a difficult task and a fine line to manage—but that is where the artistry of management comes in, and how it complements the organization's purpose, and the importance of your position.

The Importance of Mission

Hopefully your organization's mission statement translates into something everyone can truly believe and identify with. It should be all-inclusive, establishing a core foundation for the delivery of services. Unfortunately, too many mission statements lie dormant on a few plagues or as an intro to the SOPs. How often and in what manner is it regularly communicated to rank and file members?

Successful companies articulate a vision with a concise, yet comprehensive mission statement and communicate it <u>effectively</u> throughout the organization. They make sure their management team is knowledgeable and committed to mission, the statement and the ideals that comprise it, and are communicated to <u>all</u> employees <u>frequently</u>. It is one thing to create a motto or slogan like "To Protect and Serve," but more important to regularly communicate the real meaning of the principles and values underlying that theme.

There are many cute phrases, mottos, and maxims out there, i.e., Fidelity, Bravery, Integrity for the FBI, to Protect and Serve, Professionalism and Integrity, and other aphorisms emblazoned on patrol cars, entrances, plaques, etc. But seldom is the meaning of these mission-oriented maxims woven into the day to day communication between management and employees. In two surveys personally conducted at the FBI's National Academy 20 years apart, less than twenty percent of respondents in each survey felt their organization either had an effective or successfully communicated mission statement.

If your organization lacks a clear mission, then it may be up to you to identify the principles and values that underlie the organization's purpose, and communicate them effectively. Plan to regularly communicate this important theme in a variety of ways to make them substantive rather than superficial. It should be part of your regimen as a manager. In other words, because it doesn't exist officially, doesn't mean it couldn't be done by the manager that sees it as an important part of the process. *As an example, the supervisor who would frequently mention, "Our job is to investigate violations of Federal law, don't let anything else get in the way."*

Studies have shown that while pay and benefits contribute to employee satisfaction, it is still the intangible elements of respect and appreciation that mean the most. Employees need to sense what they do is connected and important to a common purpose, and keeping mission an important part of their work routine helps to create and keep that connection.

Belief #3: The Importance of Public Trust

We hear the term on occasion, but mostly as an afterthought to some news article pertaining to the arrest or indictment of a public official. It is unfortunate this principle, one which is seldom espoused in any formal sense, gets aired mostly under negative circumstance. That's because it is somewhat difficult to articulate and fully understand. *In democratic societies there is a fine line to be drawn between a necessary and healthy dose of wariness and the degree of trust afforded government to do its job.* Representative government—where the "public" elects, empowers, and allows a select few to carry out the responsibility of governing their lives depends greatly on this very important principle. It is important for sustaining the equilibrium between the government and its constituents. However, while the concept of public trust may seem somewhat nebulous or esoteric as most ideals are, the implications are very real for the public employee.

When explored further one soon realizes how this principle *could* be considered almost sacred as it is sometimes described in the occasional lapse. It is the underlying theme behind everyone's quest for life, liberty, and pursuit of happiness. It is essential to our constitutional form of governing, and the foundation of law and order that enables us to realize that ideal probably more than any other country on earth. *All anyone has to do is examine those countries without a trusted government and see the disquietude and oppression that prevails.* Public trust should be considered inviolable (sacrosanct) because of its importance to everyone in their everyday life—<u>whether they know it or not</u>.

Most people assume it is there generally, but it is only when tested that the power of this principle comes to bear. (How a department handles any kind of controversy that challenges its commitment to honesty and openness will either reinforce or severely damage this principle). It lies at the very heart of how effective any law enforcement agency will be.

This may sound overly sentimental to those working in adversarial environments where the public's reception of your service seems overly skeptical or downright hostile. However, it is still a valid principle when applied to the "whole" of law enforcement responsibility. In other words, your actions <u>wherever</u> they occur can extend beyond your immediate environment to all of law enforcement. Actions taken in defense of a fellow employee who is wrong can create the appearance of stonewalling or a cover up. This not only chips away at the department's reputation and standing in the community, but—under certain circumstances—impacts all of law enforcement and beyond. So, public trust is an important belief to keep in mind when doing what you do and holding others accountable to the same big picture understanding. It's part of your management role.

A long list of important moral principles and values like honesty, commitment, openness, and fairness etc., underlies the concept of public trust. A civil servant—as public employees are often labeled—is defined as a person employed in the public sector based on professional merit and <u>examination</u>. And, the *merit* of any professional will stem from the public's perception of one's commitment to that long list of moral values.

A trusting public on the other hand depends on hope, faith, and the expectation that public officials will perform accordingly. While it's naive to think just faith and hope is sufficient to maintain anyone's trust in government, there are a few processes in place that help bolster those expectations. Three keys for enhancing public trust are (1) <u>transparency</u> (aided by Freedom of Information access to public records and the existence of an independent press) and (2) <u>oversight</u> (from Congressional hearings, inspectors general, special prosecutors, etc., to local internal affairs systems). The third key involves oaths of office and sworn testimony. *One of the main missions of Congress is to ensure the public's trust in our government institutions. While that may sound like an oxymoron, they help do this through public hearings and oversight committees and processes. State legislatures, local commissions, and internal affairs processes also exist—in part—for that reason.*

While the principle of public trust applies to <u>all</u> government entities, there can be a discernible difference between "elected" officials, and those "hired" to actually provide the service of government. While this may imply the unfortunate view of a double standard, it still doesn't lessen the importance of holding public trust as an important part of one's management role.

There seems to be a cynical resignation by many that elected officials often ignore principle and rework certain values for political gain or survival. That being said, it is important to remember the onus for public trust falls largely on those actually delivering the public service. One can differ with and doubt an elected official, yet still have faith in those employed to fulfill the responsibility of government.

The complex nature of party politics may allow some leeway for elected officials *There are instances where discredited, even indicted officials were reelected to office.* However, the same does not hold for those appointed or hired who carry out the day-to-day requirements of government service. Elected officials get vetted through rigorous campaigns that "hopefully" reveal inconsistencies or issues in their background that voters can accept or reject. However, important civil service positions—as in law enforcement—undergo comprehensive background checks and rigorous training to determine their eligibility and, more important, their suitability to hold such an important position of public trust.

It can be argued a law enforcer's impact on individual lives is greater than that of any other public official. Nowhere in the public service realm can the relationship between citizen and government mean more in times of stress and discomfort. While it is incumbent on all public institutions to uphold the public's trust, it falls on police officers to enforce the framework of our social order with direct, personal, sometimes intimate, and very visible impact. This is why law enforcement will always seem to have the greater burden of this very unique and important concept.

The level of trust citizens have in their police department will ultimately determine the extent to which they will help (cooperating to solve crime, maintaining order, etc.), and support (increasing budgets, granting additional authority, etc.) to fulfill a department's needs. Those who hold the public's trust must work hard to ensure this important perception is maintained with consistency and validity. Without this sense of trust, public order begins to break down.

What Can Go Wrong?

How does this guiding light of public service get bent around backwards—so that it somehow becomes a platform for personal benefit? How does one get off track and veer into the gutter of trash politics, personal gain, and acts of crime? More often than not, it is a flaw that accompanies the person into public office and also the company one keeps while there. These are some of the reasons one's background and oversight is so important to the public trust and why appreciating and, yes, accommodating a free and purposely intrusive press is so important, as well.

Compromise and problem solving dilemmas, along with the subterfuge of political intrigue, can challenge the power of this principle. However, when one's sworn oath to public service begins to erode towards personal gain, abuse of power, or retribution of any kind, then failing this important belief and commitment can become a betrayal of the worse kind.

Something to Remember

The stigma for violating this almost sacred principle can be harsher for law enforcers than any other kind of endeavor or career. Like a dishonorable discharge from the service, it's a long way to fall from the grace of this high ideal to that of a discredited public servant. It is a blemish that can never be erased from one's conscience. *The disdain for a convicted law enforcer carries greater vilification than most other public service failings.* That's because of the damage it does not only to the honor of the profession generally, but how it spills over to and makes harder the job of former colleagues. *A wrongful injury, arrest, or conviction of a citizen does much damage to this principle as it relates to the whole of law enforcement.* So, yes, public trust is a huge responsibility and ideal that should be frequently pondered and touted, and demands the highest level of persistent, honest endeavor. Keeping public trust important to subordinates is part of your management role.

Belief #4: Achieving Purpose Through Others

What you want done, others must do.

Getting things done <u>through others</u> and managing change are two big benchmarks of a manager. Ensuring *purpose* gets done is the manager's responsibility, but it must be understood that what gets done will happen <u>through others</u>—especially those employees actually producing the goods, providing the service, and doing the delivery. How well subordinates perform will determine the extent of <u>your</u> contribution to the organization's purpose. *It could be argued that you need subordinates more than they need you.* It is common sense to believe that people will perform best when everything is in sync—where group and organizational equilibrium allows employees to focus and carry out what has to be done. You're going to have to work to keep that balance in place. *Subordinates are the ones actually enforcing the law, keeping the peace. They're rowing the boat. Your role is to set the pace and direct them to calmer waters ahead.*

When employee discontent from both internal and external social, political, or economic conditions bear down on your role, how do you balance the equation and keep things going during crises?

Communication is the key:

Numbers don't reveal the whole story. A manager has to know what is going on in his/her area of responsibility behind the statistics. Statistics don't create crucibles, it is what goes on behind them—the human discourse that drives the greatest challenge one may ever face. People who are bullied or offended by a peer, or know of misdeeds or potential danger areas, are not visible in bottom line figures. Yes, the job may be getting done statistically, but real problems could be percolating just beneath the surface. All the success in the world can be stained by a single disgruntled employee doing something that explodes into the public realm through a lawsuit, whistle blowing, or act of violence.

Managers aware of larger implications and complications arising from individual behavior are those who can *see* beyond the immediacy of events and include the larger picture into their decision making. That snide or sexist remark or action may be more serious than the immediate reaction indicates. When do quirks, mild eccentricities, local neighborhood banter cross the line to bullying, coercion, or insensitivity that requires intervention? *Kidding about each other's ethnicity may be a commonly accepted form of interplay in some neighborhoods or towns, but is it acceptable in the workplace?* It should be an issue you see as one part of a larger concern that may require greater intervention <u>now</u> to avoid a bigger problem later. If you were once part of that social interplay, as a manager you must rise out of the mix and stay professional. *"That's okay boss, you can call me Reb for short."* It will be best to refrain from that invitation and get used to addressing everyone by their proper name.

Respect and civility help to resolve problems without producing another set of issues or conflicts. It requires engaging an open and broad based line of communication that can discover issues <u>before</u> they become a more serious problem.

Impromptu, indirect, ad-hoc channels of communication are an important part of a manager's ability to know what is going on with subordinates. It doesn't happen by touting an open door policy and never leaving the office (*waiting for them to come to you*). Subordinates are much more open to those who develop and nurture these channels, and lie hidden from those who fail to actively engage them. (*You've got to go to them.*) It may be a lousy term, but be sure to spend time in *enemy territory*. Crash the party; intrude into the clique or coalition of supporters, which can sometimes surround a disgruntled problem employee. Be sure to engage him, her, or them on a regular basis. Avoid "avoidance."

Managers who engage employees often in non-threatening, instructional, encouraging ways are most likely to build the kind of trust that helps subordinates share information. This means not visiting a component or patrol sector <u>only</u> when there is a problem, but dropping by on occasion to express interest and appreciation—management by walking around. Engage employees, talk to them, and take an interest in what they do—even those you may not like personally. Solicit their opinions or ideas on how to make their assignment more effective, etc. *If you do it for one, best do it for all.* Be attentive to what's going on in their lives. A personalized note recognizing an accomplishment or special event <u>always</u> means a lot to subordinates, and even the problem employee, too. *Remember, an occasional deserved recognition of a problem employee doesn't mitigate their problem performance or impinge your efforts to document or discipline. It shows fairness as a manager and bolsters your position regarding actions taken to correct a problem.*

If you are uncomfortable with being a people person, try to learn to like them anyway, and have faith in their abilities. Look at people objectively—apart from whatever bias or belief you may have about human nature. Try to believe that most want to do things right. Also, don't forget to assess management's role in the problem. Is it possible <u>you</u> may be part of the problem, too (shirking accountability, avoiding unpleasant or awkward situations, or requiring too little or too much)? All this helps to develop a personal orientation designed to make you more influential, as opposed to just maintaining status quo (inconsequential), or downright inhibiting. **It helps *others* do better what needs to be done.**

Belief #5: You must also manage change.

An old adage has three kinds of people in this world: Those who make things happen, those who watch what happens, and those who <u>wonder</u> what happened. In today's fast paced environment one can't afford to just watch or wonder … You have to get out ahead of it— and stay there!

Change is a huge factor in today's fast paced, sometimes instantaneous environment. Newly enacted federal and state laws, new inventions, change in management personnel and/or philosophy, are some of the major technological, social, and political change that can wreak havoc on any work environment.

Technology and social media have expanded communication and changed the face of human interaction in ways many find hard to understand. Mainstreaming diverse cultural, handicapped, and lifestyle needs, moderating or deflecting external and internal stresses to the work force is the reality of the "role" of a modern manager. It often disrupts the comfort zone of entrenched employees, and the natural reaction by some is to resist. <u>You</u> may be uncomfortable with the change, too. It's not just a matter of "Well, that's the law—live with it," and then react to issues when they arise. Successful change agents get out ahead of a situation by seeking to understand it from a larger perspective, and then "work the crowd" (*informing, educating*) in order to effectively facilitate its implementation. *Once a controversial program or initiative is mandated by upper-management, the supervisor must either sign on or get out of the way.*

Any action to disparage or prevent the process will undermine your proper role. Besides, one never knows, you could be wrong in your assessment.

Change can be viewed in two ways. You can watch it happen and re-act to its impact. Or, try to understand its realistic implications for the future and get ahead of it. The latter view will help lessen resistance and better facilitate its inevitability in a less problematic way. It's entirely up to you—how you choose to perceive it. Instant Messaging, Facebook, iPhones, Twitter, etc.—may require one to think about ways to harness this reality and use it, or ways to effectively manage it, as opposed to shoveling against a tide with efforts to ban or punish for it.

How to Institute Change

One must make an honest effort to truly understand whatever is being changed. As a law enforcer you've been trained to methodically and persistently investigate criminality. One should apply the same principles to the change you are facing. You may not agree with a company work-at-home policy, a revised patrol configuration, or a newly devised program to monitor emails and or office twitters, etc. *An alien entity like a motor vehicle department enforcement group is being absorbed into your agency, and you are strongly opposed to it. You've looked at it, voiced your opposing reasons to upper management, but they have decided to go with it anyway for efficiency and budgetary reasons. Do you continue to fight it, or do what is necessary to facilitate its implementation by working to adjust its capability to your standards and expectations?* The effective role model will strive to know what drives the policy, understand it from a comprehensive perspective, and advise whatever reservations or suggestions you have directly to its author(s). Then—if enacted—set the example by committing yourself to its implementation, and engage employees in a way that educates and influences them to do likewise. If there is a continuing legitimate policy dispute that may—as an example— jeopardize safety for financial efficiency, then it must be addressed directly with its authors through appropriate channels and in a professional manner. Voicing to subordinates your own disgruntle- ment or opposition to a change for the sake of old relationships or misplaced sense of camaraderie <u>always</u> undermines your effectiveness.

CHAPTER 5

Acquiring the Right Orientation

Everyone reading this book is subordinate to someone else. Most managers focus on what and how subordinates should be doing something? To better comprehend your position in relation to your role, why not consider the reverse perspective? <u>What do my subordinates expect from me?</u>

To better understand what subordinates expect from their superiors, ask yourself what you expect from your boss. Even if your boss is tough and demanding, you'd want him or her to at least be civil, competent, accessible, and fair—the intangibles that constitute reasonable expectations of a professional boss.

Now ask yourself if you are providing these same qualities to your subordinates? The closer you are to the expectations subordinates have for the position, the greater validity, integrity, and influence you will have with your subordinates. This will help what needs to get done is done to the extent and manner desired. Remember, you've got to give what you expect to get in return. This realization should occur <u>before</u> the deluge of responsibility dominates your attention, shortens your time, temper, and dictates your actions.

To change any orientation, time and effort must be taken to first understand the expectations and beliefs needed in order to acquire a new perspective. It is important to understand that it's not a matter of how well you perform as it is how well your subordinates perform that will measure the degree of your success.

SOPs (a manager's responsibility) are only one part of the management equation. What you bring to bear from within will constitute most of it. Role brings all the intangibles to the fore. It is the glue *and* oil that makes your part play well—achieve more. Planning, Organizing, Staffing, Direction, Coordinating, Reporting, Budgeting are the fundamentals of what has to be done. Your personal orientation is the key to how it will get done.

Training and education help to influence orientation, but it's important to think about yourself on occasion, too. This requires introspection—to the extent you can recognize and assess your strengths and weaknesses before the inundation of PODSCoRB takes control of your day. Ask yourself, will SOPs be driving you, or will you be driving them?

It's time for some deeply personal questions. What do you want from both yourself and the position? Articulate what you feel. Are you basically distrustful? Do you like to engage others, or prefer the solitude of your own thoughts? How open are you to new ideas and suggestions? Can you see beyond what is directly in front of you and comprehend a larger picture? How can I enhance my interpersonal skills? Can you see the difference between what your area of responsibility currently is and what it *should* be? If you sense or truly recognize a personal deficiency, is it possible to change? How does one go about acquiring or enhancing the interpersonal skills and abilities that are expected for the position? How can I rejuvenate and sustain the ideals and beliefs that first attracted me to this profession?

You may be confident in your knowledge of what the agency expects with regard to rules and regulations, etc. Then think about what *you* must do to be more effective interpersonally. Write yourself a letter. It will help set up and structure your personal orientation. *I believe in the legitimacy and mission of my employer and the oath I've sworn. I must improve in the following areas, etc.* Then buy into it, believe it, and keep the letter handy—refer to it often. Let it serve as the compass for your management persona.

Remember, your management role is to effectively handle challenge and change in support of a common purpose (mission) through the efforts of others. It's much more than just managing functional responsibilities. It includes understanding the role you must fill in support of a mission, and getting subordinates to buy into it as well. <u>If they do their job as it should be done, then you've done yours.</u>

CHAPTER 6

Committing to Role

Reorienting views takes a comprehensive effort. A good manager will consciously accept and fulfill the bottom line subordinate expectations, and assimilate the beliefs that underlie the position he or she holds. These are qualities a manager needs to nurture and develop just as much as daily responsibilities. It will involve an ongoing effort to improve competency, communication skills, and sometimes physical stamina. A good start would be to:

- Decide to BE a manager, and make it a continuous learning process.

- Choose respected colleagues as role models—and keep thinking about yourself and assessing your progress.

- Read, read, and read more management related books and articles. Take courses in management. Don't ever underestimate the need for you to change—to grow into each position. It should be a continuous educational process—one of the foundations for making _you_ a strong role model.

- Make an honest effort to re-value and suppress personal bias or feelings regarding prior perceptions—so that you can acquire greater tolerance and flexibility. This will determine how comfortable you'll be with the extent of responsibility imposed by the organization and any changes it undergoes. It will also assist in getting ahead of issues instead of always reacting to them.

This helps evolve a "force" of personality because you now know the full extent of "what it is" you *should* be doing. Force of personality influences subordinates in such a way that the group's attachment and enthusiasm for the leader and mission inadvertently improves the performance of marginal peers. Group focus shifts more to mission and the leader's influence, and becomes less tolerant of problem employee shenanigans.

Role elevates your awareness, expands your influence, and enhances your overall effectiveness. It becomes the force within you.

Role: How to know it and use it

Your role is not only to manage functional job responsibilities, but to *believe* in the nobility of your position, the importance of a common purpose, and the public's trust. You must accept the challenge to facilitate change, and recognize that the mission will be accomplished mostly through the efforts of your subordinates—not you. And, it will best be done by meeting subordinate expectations in a respectful, civil, competent, fair, trusting, and courageous manner. Whew!

You are not being promoted to play a part. You are being tasked with the most important role in the whole production—the first line supervisor. It is the management role closest to the most important component in the organization—those actually providing the service directly to the public.

1. <u>Get to know yourself</u> and how you fit your role. Management is a noble calling. Believe it! Think about yourself from a professional perspective. Elevate its value to you personally and professionally. Incorporate your role's basic principles and values into your daily repertoire of action.

2. Assume the proper demeanor of your position. Realize you are there to support the mission, achieve goals, and meet objectives <u>through others</u>. Help fulfill what most subordinates expect by affording them the direction, support, access, and recognition that will fuel their commitment and devotion to their job requirements.

3. Maximize this capability by creating an environment that garners the respect, dignity, opportunity, safety, and equal application of your time and attention.

4. <u>Revisit these basic ideals and rejuvenate them daily</u>. Think about yourself and your role. Day to day obligations and issues can cloud their relevance to what you do. This is the role you must fill—that maximizes the part you play. It makes the lines and verses you read come to life and makes your part mean so much more to others. This happens when management's role and your persona come together for maximum effectiveness.

It's a big challenge, much more difficult than just playing the part, but so much more effective and fulfilling when achieved.

PART II

EXPLORING

YOUR

BOTTOM LINE

When principle and values collide:

We are all basically attuned to honesty.

Honesty is more than a value. As a society we
accept honesty—in principle—as an important
part of our heritage and baseline of social need.
Values are a personal choice—we choose
whether or not and to what extent we will be loyal
or friendly to someone or thing.

CHAPTER 7

Exploring Your "Bottom Line"
(Where a well meaning manager can go terribly wrong)

The ultimate test (crucible) of any manager's bottom line will usually revolve around the strong forces of and a conflict between the principle of **Honesty** and two of the most highly regarded values in our culture—**Friendship and Loyalty**.

Shredding a document in defense of your agency's reputation. Ignoring, stifling, even avenging a whistle blower's complaint. Overlooking a friend's malfeasance. "Shading" a response to an official inquiry. All are examples of actions taken by well meaning managers in the heat of conflict, which can erupt between the principle of honesty, and the values of loyalty and friendship.

The closer you are to your subordinates and peers, and committed to your career and company, the more friendship and loyalty can weigh heavily into how you react to an ominously litigable and potentially career-ending challenge. Friendship and loyalty can create quandaries, which can propel you in ways you never thought possible. When an incident or controversy escalates to a point where it could jeopardize careers, friends, reputation, or freedom for a highly valued someone or something else—**will you make the *right* choice for the right reason?**

<u>Some Good People Have Not</u>

In the heat of controversy, when responding to lawful sources of authority while confronting their own fears and bias, desperate pleas or cajoling of friends, and/or a skewered sense of obligation—they chose to do what they thought was right in the heat of the moment, but later discovered it was for the wrong reason. **What will you do and will it be for all the right reasons?**

What is a bottom line?

A bottom line is a moral boundary you have decided to *never* cross under <u>any</u> circumstance *regardless* of the consequences! It is the "line in the sand" that prepares you to lose the deal or a friendship; it allows someone guilty to go free or risks damage to your cause. It is the line you draw for the sake of a moral stance that will ultimately protect your integrity and sense of well being, and what will likely be *everyone's* long term best interest.

However, how many are truly aware of their bottom line <u>when</u> they need to know it, which is usually at the outset of whatever issue is creating the crucible? (*A crucible is a career defining test that portends severe consequences*). Thankfully, most managers are. However, for some it is a question of how to balance their responsibility and commitment to their position and the law with the emotional realm of longstanding associations and relationships?

Civil rights violations comprise an area with too many examples of cohorts and supervisors exacerbating an issue by doing something devious or obstructionist. It is often done in the name of loyalty and friendship, and/or because of a negative bias towards the internal function or outside agency responsible for its resolution. In many situations the initial incident was <u>not</u> the reason for the eventual crucible. It's what happened *after* that made it so much more sinister or conspiratorial—post incident maneuvering (*changing reports, omitting pertinent information when asked, purposely overlooking or altering evidence, contriving other scenarios, etc.*) by employees protecting each other for all the wrong reasons.

For the sake of argument, we'll avoid the value of self-preservation. Although one could argue it is the same as being loyal to oneself, it can be assumed good managers are people of character who put moral principles above their own comfort—who are oriented to do right. It's when a misconstrued and undeserving sense of noble sacrifice puts another above your own welfare and what you know is right, that the bottom line should play its most crucial role.

Smart versus not-so-much!

It is amazing how certain personalities can spend their lives being smart and then risk it all on one stupid act. Sports figures are a prime example: The amount of time, discipline, blood, sweat, and luck, which got them into the major league, where they attained fame, respect, wealth, and sense of satisfaction, but then *flittered* it away. It was the one illegal bet, one too many drinks, an underage paramour, steroid use, or whatever inappropriate circumstance they may have known was wrong—but did it anyway.

The same rationale can be applied to law enforcement officers. They spend their formative years staying on the straight and narrow, behaving in a way that allows them to pass a comprehensive background check, overcome the rigors of a training academy to build—over time—a reputation that champions a great career. And yet, there are examples of reputable and very competent people who inexplicably jump into stupid for what ultimately was a momentary libidinous urge and lapse of judgment.

How does it happen?

Smart people consider the larger picture when faced with temptation to engage in unnecessary or career destroying risk. The not-so-smart let the emotion of the moment—the lascivious or compelling character flaw—override the rational as well as the existence of a larger time frame for their lives. It's like putting your entire life on one number at the craps table. They allow themselves to be bullied, badgered, or sucked into something they may sense is wrong, and then cross what should have been their bottom line. For managers, it is often misguided loyalty or misunderstood friendship can compel that kind of mistake. .

So, before you stick your neck out for anyone doing wrong or for an unworthy cause, before you risk your career and sense of self respect, it's a good idea to explore some of the reasons why. It is important to become familiar *with your* bottom line <u>before</u> you face the crucible that will test it all.

These are the friendly words of potential wrongs—"*just between you and me, cover for me, keep this under your hat, let it slide, no one will ever know, get with the program, could you change this, it's their word against ours, you owe me,* etc., etc." Any of these phrases should be the alarm bell of your bottom line. They should startle you into complete focus on the issue at hand. They usually imply an issue is approaching a "No Trespass" zone secured by your knowledge of and appreciation for the rule of law and its practical application to everything managers do.

Without fully understanding what loyalty and/or friendship really are or should be, and how they can compete with honesty, one may say and do something that mitigates the immediate issue, but later proves to be a choice resulting in greater unexpected consequences. This is especially true when a friend or organization is threatened by what <u>one</u>

may erroneously consider an unfair, unnecessary, or politically suspicious challenge. It's important to understand your position in relation to honesty, loyalty, and friendship *before* you're forced to sort them out in the heat of controversy.

The problem:

Product culpability and service responsibilities have inherent risks that can become major controversies at the drop of a hat. In other words, someone has done something wrong, and as a manager you're about to become either part the problem or its resolution—like it or not!

We are an intensely litigious society. The courts and their ancillary processes have become the main arena for resolving personnel, product, and delivery disputes throughout our modern work environment. Public service jobs carry the greater burden of a trust that includes a myriad of monitors and regulators to ensure <u>everyone's</u> interests are protected. Oaths of office, special investigative entities, internal affairs, human resource oversight, and other processes are the catalysts for pushing honesty, loyalty and friendship into conflict. As a manager you are increasingly liable for the actions of your subordinates. Internal administrative actions and/or criminal investigations can entangle you even if you haven't been directly involved with whatever is at issue.

Media and legal access to information is expanding faster today than at any time in history. Means of communication have evolved dramatically along with inherent vulnerabilities to your everyday actions. Email, text messaging, twitter, widespread video presence all raise the risks to what you say and do—especially with regard to what you've previously said and done.

In law enforcement *anything* can become a catalyst for career ending mistakes. That's because much of the work involves a wide range of emotionally charged endeavors. There are tough environments out there where the distance between what is necessary and preferable is quite wide; neighborhoods where adversity, lawlessness, and confrontation is prevalent. They reek of cynicism and distrust, and force officers into a defensive mode. And yet, it is this kind of environment where the importance of one's understanding of role and bottom line are most important.

From compromise to decisive (sometimes instantaneous) actions, and later analysis and adjudication, the principle of honesty and its relationship to loyalty and friendship can be a compelling and challenging part of everyday life. That's because enforcing the law demands a high degree of bonding and reliance on each other, which greatly intensifies the influence of loyalty and friendship. It can be a real quandary for a new manager when challenged with an issue bearing harsh consequences for those you know and like.

Many law enforcement agencies have internal affairs (IA) processes that are viewed by rank and file members with mistrust. They suspect IA motives and its ability to perform competently and fairly. Suspicions of political subterfuge can propel an urge to be overly cautious or less than fully cooperative. It could become a damage control situation—the need to contain the truth, prevent it from being blown out of proportion, or mishandled by those you suspect can't or won't see it as it should be seen. *"They" (whoever is asking) don't understand or appreciate the dynamics or reality of your situation, therefore are not legitimate in your mind.* Sometimes what *you* may think are minor circumstances (*two friends of differing ethnicity joke about each other's heritage, a common occurrence in your sector*) become more serious than expected or what *you* may think is warranted.

These are just some of the perceptions that can generate a "me versus them" perspective or an "employee versus management" position, both of which can give rise to strong defensive postures (circling of wagons) that loyalty and friendship can induce. There are too many examples of instinctive responses to official questions that must be corrected or retracted at a later, more serious stage.

In law enforcement it is often called the "blue wall." It is a phenomenon embedded in the clash between important values—namely the emotion laden power of friendship and loyalty thrust up against the more rational forces of honesty and the law. It is an unscripted code of silence and conscious obstruction to thwart efforts by a legitimate authority to resolve an act or suspicion of wrongdoing, which bears probable negative consequences for the subject of their inquiry. A blue wall can consist of two individuals or hundreds, but it impacts how a supervisor can be pushed beyond their bottom line.

However, regardless of its origin or how you perceive it, **any issue that requires documentation, official interviews, testimony, and statements under oath, should be strongly embedded in your "bottom line."**

The dilemma:

The adversarial nature of daily interaction with the public becomes the foundation for cynicism and hardness that can massage values in ways few people experience outside the realm of police work. Any kind of bottom line can get blurred as officers watch what they once perceived as core values being manipulated and cast aside in so many ways. The incredible diversity of experiences that impact a police officer's role requires a great deal of discretion—the flexibility to respond to nebulous and out-of-the-box issues that form the basis of law and order and keeping the peace. Good doesn't always win the

battle between right and wrong. Survival and operational effectiveness may require an officer to employ tactics some consider unsavory
and less than honest—false pretense interviews, aggressive interrogation, quasi or official undercover roles, or resolving impossible domestic issues.

This reality raises the bar for loyalty and friendship when an officer's
actions are revisited for clarification or adjudication by another lawful
authority. It could pressure officers to pick and choose between honesty, loyalty, and friendship in ways no other occupation demands
with such direct and damaging consequences.

This section is designed to help managers avoid the pitfalls friendship
and loyalty can pose for honesty when responding to legitimate reviews or inquiries. In other words, how to avoid surpassing what you
later find should have been your bottom line. It is more than just
knowing right from wrong. **It is a matter of doing what is right
while dealing with a wrong.**

What is a crucible?

Any kind of response to even a quasi-official review that involves
lack of candor or outright lies immediately opens the door to a crucible. A crucible is more than a test. It is a quandary forced by a lawful
inquiry for information you have that may involve serious
consequences for something or someone you know and like. It grows
out of a fact or allegation that either someone or a group you value
highly failed to uphold a moral or lawful expectation. The failure is
under review and requires your input. The review could involve dire
consequences for you, those you know, the organization, or an ideal
you may value. In most cases, a crucible pits either or both friendship
and loyalty against your obligation and devotion to honesty—the
foundation of the "true faith and allegiance, uphold and defend," or

whatever else constitutes the public service oath you have *solemnly* sworn yourself to bear …

The driving force behind this conflict will be the monitoring or enforcement entity that is lawfully sanctioned to address the issue. It could be a cursory management inquiry, internal affairs, another law enforcement agency, legislative panel, special prosecutor, or other oversight function.

In many cases it is after "mismanagement" by management that an issue becomes a crucible. For example, a whistle blower (WB) can present a real quandary—regardless of how you view their legitimacy or intent. *WBs are better protected legally against ill conceived reactions by management than they were in the past.* Some make heroic efforts to surface wrongdoing they know will have dire consequences for themselves, the organization, and their colleagues. However, you may surmise they are less loyal, more self-serving, or suspect disgruntlement, retaliation, or some other inappropriate motive.

In spite of your inclinations to believe the WB one way or the other, one must make a real effort to weigh their own views objectively. What are the <u>facts</u>? Although it is appropriate to afford the benefit of doubt, it is irresponsible to automatically assume that doubt is fact; and it is absolutely wrong to contrive an intervention to marginalize or defeat the claim, or to intimidate or retaliate against the whistle blower that *now* makes <u>you</u> part of the problem.

Crucibles test the very core of one's character—the centerpiece of any professional persona. Character is the constant in the storm of everyone's life, the inner voice that rises above the din of everyday foibles to keep one focused on the principles and the hierarchy of values you hold. *It must not be confused with personality. Personality is a vehicle by which we communicate character. There are great personalities with little character.* It will test your mettle as well, the courage and resolve to

<u>stay true to character </u>(what you believe to be right) as the intensity of the process and the consequences of the issue rise in severity.

What do you value?

Values are personal preferences shaped during our formative years by an unlimited number of experiences and influences (family, friends, neighborhood, education, social status, religious affiliation, work experience, exposure to media, etc). They influence both perception and behavior, and how you relate to and interact with your environment. Values evolve into a hierarchy that will be similar to those held by others in any common cultural or social setting, but when analyzed individually make us unique from one another. *Other, more self-serving values like ambition, immediate gratification, wealth, greed, etc., drive people in powerful ways, too. However, when <u>well meaning managers</u> make mistakes handling serious controversies, they often result from the quandary of having to choose between loyalty, friendship, and honesty.* Which value do you rank above another, and what higher principle or outcome would compel you to change what you think is your greatest preference?

Exploring these Values

As discussed earlier in understanding Role, principles are fundamental laws or doctrine. They serve as guiding lights for our sense of right and wrong. The principle for being honest can be a real spoiler for loyalty and friendship, which are more emotional, subjective, and tenuous values.

We each have needs and desires, which are powerful forces influencing what we see, say, and do. Many psychologists recognize a basic human craving for appreciation. We all need the companionship, socialization, support and recognition from friends and cohorts, and to believe in a purpose (worthy goals). The greater the intensity of this craving, the more likely one is to be influenced by values like loyalty and friendship when grappling with an issue involving severe consequences for being honest. However, within this craving for appreciation also lies an inherent deference for honesty. Our culture ingrains this inclination through a variety of religious, customary, parental, and educational means.

However, there are circumstances when honesty can be subjugated for a higher cause or outcome. For example, international diplomacy may require a less than candid approach to some issues for the sake of national security. The physical and psychological welfare of others under certain conditions is another. An undercover officer doesn't reveal his identity to his criminal cohorts for the sake of this principle, nor do we necessarily tell the whole truth to a suspect or competing entity that would give them unfair advantage. We don't share the realities of life with young children (Santa Claus, anyone?), etc.—all for the sake of something that could be considered a rational and commonly accepted higher purpose. The truth is you can't stand the person you are dealing with. However, a "higher purpose" has you tempering your actions for the sake of a more professional outcome by acting in ways that may not reflect your true feelings.

So, there are circumstances where we may compromise honesty to achieve what we think is a morally or ethically better place to be. Strong forces of camaraderie, deeply personal relationships, prior favors or promises, or even family issues can fuel friendship, loyalty and honesty with compelling reasons to choose one over the other.

How can you know which value is more "right" (righteous) than another?

"Right" is a standard that is solidly positioned within the concept of ethics and morality. It is appropriate for all the elements of an issue and applies equally to little things as well as major ones. It is the position that a moral person would consider reasonable, preferable, and justified under the circumstances—a stance that has a <u>morally defensible outcome</u>.

The reason we would choose loyalty and/or friendship over honesty is because we believe it serves a greater purpose than a true representation of the facts honesty deserve. *I chose to allow an investigator's transgressions (verbal abuse of a kidnapper or less than honest dealings with suspect's attorney) committed for the sake of overcoming an obstacle to a critically important investigation. Doing otherwise would have jeopardized a greater good (eliciting the missing victim's location and possibly save a life under time sensitive circumstances).* You subjugated a required "right" (professional protocol) for what you truly believed was a higher, more moral "right" under the circumstances.

The crucible will entail your reporting or explaining the facts truthfully as they exist, and not trying to minimize or mollify them with invention or denial. *(Falsely claiming the suspect resisted, or you didn't know what transpired.)* The honest course would be to explain the justification (intent) that prompted your actions, and not to contrive something you think will diminish possible consequences. Do not worry that others may second guess your judgment. *The above example may be an extreme case and one not normally within the purview of a first time supervisor. However, the point to be made is that when selecting loyalty to something over honesty, it better be <u>very</u> important, rationally based, and morally defensible.* It is the manager's perception of what constitutes or legitimizes a higher purpose that lies at the heart of this issue—especially when strong friendship or loyalties play a role. Are you willing to do what is right at personal cost?

The Formation of a Test

It could be an impromptu performance critique, an off-color joke that everyone seems to enjoy, a request to post date a late report, changing an amount on a voucher, an innocent or well intended embrace or touch of another, which may find you ignoring or overlooking a minor infraction. They are examples of routine and seemingly innocuous interactions with employees that take place every day. And they will stay routine until you are <u>asked to recall, explain, and expound further on what you knew, did or failed to do</u>. Then a test begins to take shape—the need to provide an answer or decide a course of action that has you weighing the consequences of what you said or did, or are about to say or do. It can turn routine into something serious.

The Test—Plus Two!

There are many challenges managers face during each day. Compromise becomes a necessary tool in handling competing or difficult issues. Many have no simple or definitive solutions. How we choose to handle them becomes part of a "**<u>history of action</u>**"—what gets recorded and/or observed by others. No one can be correct <u>all</u> the time. What we intended on the one hand can always be questioned on the other. Your initial action(s) may be questionable, even risky under the circumstances, but it's what you do (intent) when questioned about it later that becomes the framework for a crucible. *Intent is a key word. It strikes at the heart of this dilemma—the individual's inclination to do what is proper and justified versus reckless, devious, or illegal.*

It is when "what you did or didn't do" comes under greater scrutiny by a more official interest that the values of loyalty or friendship can seep into your decision making rationale. It's where managers get tested <u>twice</u>. **Once**, when you first observe the act, learn of the wrongdoing, entertain the request, and decide your course of action, **and again** when you are asked about it during a review or official inquiry.

What you did initially is now part of a "history" of your actions, and how you choose to relate that action to an administrative demand or official inquiry is another. It becomes a double whammy for managers where serious consequences could be part of the mix. *An officer purposely exceeds the use of force doctrine, and other officers help cover up the violation. An admired superior removes references to safety concerns raised by subordinates in a report to be submitted to a regulatory commission. You hear of or witness a close friend and associate commit an unethical or illegal act to achieve a desired end—"fudging" evidence or lying on the stand to achieve a conviction of a despicable subject. A subordinate surfaces a wrongdoing that threatens group equilibrium and the welfare of the organization? A star employee is accused of sexual harassment by a less valued employee, and their actions are now under review.* You feel an urge to protect who or whatever is in peril out of friendship or loyalty, which could include concern for the department's image or welfare.

The problem may be you didn't handle the initial test very well. You overlooked, ignored, or forgot to take appropriate action with the issue or question. Or, you made the mistake of what some call "redlining," or "just this once" syndrome. I'll do it (lie, fib, ignore, forget, etc.) out friendship or loyalty just this once and never again. However, once done it becomes a slippery slope if others become aware: "Well, you did it for him, why not for me?"

The crucible becomes the test of the unexpected. What you originally thought was a minor issue has now become a major one. *You overhear, yet ignore, a dispatcher failing to respond properly to a 911 call, and it's later learned a fatality was the result.* It could be a mistake or conscious violation of rules or ethics by one of your subordinates that now has you directly in the line of fire; and your input may involve harsh consequences.

Why didn't you document that incident? Why didn't you mention that mistake to us earlier? Why didn't you take proper action at the time? Suddenly, it is test time—mulling the choice of one value over another for the sake of what may be the wrong reasons.

The Lure of Excuses: Avoidance

Avenues of excuses can appear out of nowhere. They are dead-end streets paved with temptation to contrive other scenarios you think will lessen probable consequences. It may have one refuting what they've said or done, diverting blame, or reworking circumstances to fit a new (less consequential) view of the problem.

The manager who ignores blatant wrong doing or fails to provide applicable information at an official inquiry does it more from an emotional urge than a rational choice. Excuses are only an escape route from taking responsibility for your actions—even minor ones. Here is where knowing your bottom line comes in handy.

Bottom Lines to Consider

When any issue involves either a quasi or official status, there should be nothing that would compel you to choose another value above what you know to be true—a boundary beyond which no higher purpose exists. This happens when one incorporates the following "Bottom Line" factors into their supervisory persona:

1) **One will not fabricate, invent, delete, omit, or ignore required information for <u>any</u> reason in the execution of their duties, no matter how trivial, self serving, singular, or convenient it may seem.** This may seem to be part of your normal persona, but the circumstances

in which they get tested during a crucible are not normal. *"Can you post date this report? It's only a day late."* The consequence for a delayed report submission may be the officer has to write a report about why it is late. Post dating may help the officer avoid this minor administrative consequence and make you a "good guy" in his or her eyes, but don't forget that making him or her suffer that inconvenience <u>now</u> may help them do it right next time. More importantly, it also communicates your bottom line commitment to truth and responsibility in <u>all</u> matters, which could dissuade future attempts to seek your *help* in a more serious wrong.

2) **<u>Never</u> omit or shade information, or lie while <u>under oath in court, hearing, deposition, or other officially sworn proceeding</u>**—*let the chips fall where they may.* Intensely loyal but more chaotic or loosely managed environments, where paranoia, quasi-legal actions, and unhealthy conflict exist, can induce this kind of predicament. For some, a bottom line may be a last resort kind of stance. *Previous statements to lesser venues lacked complete candor, but now it is court time.* A court of law should be everyone's <u>absolute</u> bottom line—regardless of the environment, predicament, circumstances, or consequences.

3) **One should never add to one mistake with another** is an additional bottom line rule to remember. This equation never results in a better outcome. It only deepens the seriousness of the issue at hand.

4) Also, **it's seldom too late to correct whatever wrong has occurred**. At what point should it be apparent that something you thought was handled in a less than

preferable manner is not going away, and is actually compounding the consequences? One should always question what is driving the current course of action. *Circumstances lie at the heart of the issue, and most mistaken decisions are based on partial and likely biased information.* So, the next logical bottom line consideration should be:

5) **Muster all the facts of the situation before deciding any course of action.** And this doesn't just include facts of the incident, but your views of whom and why the situation is being revisited. Ask questions, <u>get the facts</u>.

Remember, each of these bottom lines must be backed by a <u>very strong</u> resolve to accept whatever consequences may result. You want to maintain the balance between the challenge of your crucible and deeply held convictions that serve as the basis of your sense of self respect and equilibrium. In other words, what you <u>know</u> is right.

The Highest Value

We are a nation of laws and most try to abide by them. They help serve as the foundation to our sense of right and wrong. It should be the anchor holding steady amongst an overload of compromise and accommodation that gets us through a day filled with chaos, tension, resistance, and change.

Consistently engaging a bottom line communicates a clear sense of "boundary" for what is right. A well advertised bottom line may very well dissuade others from broaching or cajoling any kind of impropriety later—because they know from previous experience where your boundary lies. It creates a good foundation for weathering controversy and conflict.

Ask yourself:

Does the activity I am documenting, recording, or reporting reflect the factual occurrence of the event, or am I misrepresenting something in the name of what may be misunderstood values? Am I <u>consciously</u> omitting or failing to do something that I know is required or should be done for the same reasons? All of these situations should register at least a subconscious alert that should not be suppressed for the sake of something less honest.

In conclusion

This and the following chapters don't have all the answers. They are designed to have you think about the interrelationship between honesty, loyalty, and friendship to help you become aware of a more rational bottom line perspective. It will help keep you safe in the wonderful, but sometimes chaotic, risky, and complex world of law enforcement management. By reading the following chapters on honesty, loyalty and friendship, hopefully it will help you think about where a bottom line fits within each, and how they should be weighed in regard to the challenge you face. Hopefully, it gives you greater insight to stand ready should a crucible occur.

Remember, you are now a manager. You have a new role to play. Exploring these values <u>now</u> may give you a better perspective to re-evaluate and better understand their proper position in relation to your decision making acumen—**<u>before</u> you stick your neck out for what has you later lamenting "I wish I hadn't done or said that ..."**

CHAPTER 8

Honesty

"Once to every man and nation comes the moment to decide,
In the strife of Truth with Falsehood, for the good or evil side ..."
(James Russell Lowell, 1844)

Honesty truly is the best policy. It's an old cliché that still rings true today.

Truth is fact. It is correct, exact. Honesty has more to do with how truth is conveyed. Perception, memory, and even language can impact this principle. (Two people can witness the same event and relate it differently, both with honest intent). You are most honest when you convey something as close to the truth as possible, being faithful to the facts as they really are.

The dictionary defines honesty as free from fraud, characterized by integrity and straightforwardness in conduct and thought. It expresses absence of intent to deceive and implies candor. Synonyms include truthfulness, veracity, candor, credibility, authenticity, integrity, etc.

A reputation for being honest is a huge personal asset. It is one of the most important elements for character development and an image

from which others perceive you as trustworthy and a valued association. It builds over time and in large part from actions taken when
being honest meant disadvantage or discomfort to you. People saw
that principle stood firm versus something else employed for convenience, out of fear, or superficial self interest.

While consequences of being honest are mostly positive and
equally so for those around you, **there are situations where it can
be almost like a bomb:** It is a principle that can produce casual-
ties and what you feel must be carefully wielded (*for the good or evil
side*) in the chaos of intense controversy. *A valued employee, a long time
friend, a loyal cohort, has made a grievous error, and the urge to protect or
lessen the potential consequences lies heavy in your heart.* When truth carries
serious detrimental consequences, like the possible loss of one's
job or freedom—especially those who fit within the realm of
friend—then greater quandary and caution can enter the decision
making mix.

That's because …

When we open the hood and explore the actual working parts of
honesty, we see situations in which truth can rub up against greater
and sometimes more valid needs. We find it possible to be less than
totally honest, while still being moral or ethical, and comfortable with
our choice of action. It seems to imply a bit of wiggle room, and
there lies the quandary for anyone faced with the challenge of a
lifetime—a test that bears heavy consequences for someone or thing
of great importance to your life.

*A defense attorney outside the courtroom or reporter in casual conversation unex-
pectedly asks if someone is your informant. While saying that department policy
prohibits commenting on such matters, you feel circumstances surrounding such a
pat answer will just as likely imply that he or she is an informant. One might get*

away with a quizzical look and a "Who?" while shaking their head, but this situation may require a more shielding denial. However, when asked during an administrative inquiry or court proceeding in a controversy involving the informant, what will you do?

At what point do you go no further into the grey area of subverting honesty for the sake of something you feel compelled to do, but rationally know you shouldn't? This is especially true in the intense and chaotic landscape of policing, where discretionary choice is a key element in decision making. It is in this arena where managers should have a good sense of their "bottom line."

The Quandary

Honesty is a principle we strive to fulfill, but don't always achieve. That's because under certain conditions honesty may be somewhat malleable for the sake of a greater value or "higher" purpose. Where many go wrong is not so much with the original sin. Nobody's perfect. Everyone screws up on occasion. It's how the sinner and others react to its aftermath. How it gets "conveyed" to an entity with the power to exact consequences. *A child lies to a parent that he didn't throw the rock that broke the window. The lie becomes the greater of two wrongs— thereby increasing the probable consequences, especially as they relate to the expectations of the parent.*

It is implausible to be totally honest all the time. Aside from an occasional lapse during flirtatious exaggerations or historical embellishment, we can also fall victim to selective memory, conscious omission, or slight alteration while executing proper manners, being civil, avoiding confrontation, wrestling with conflicting or unreasonable reporting requirements, sheer weight of numbers (everyone else does it), or just plain business and political survival—"I did not have sex with that woman ..." (*President Clinton, circa 1996*)

In hopes of achieving what some would consider a higher ethical position (a rationally justified outcome) we sometimes engage a less than honest approach to take the edge off navigating the volatile shoals of human interaction. They are called little white lies or minor indiscretions. They offer an easier (what many would consider preferable or acceptable) way to avoid confrontation and conflict for what you believe is a more righteous place to be. In other words, it is possible to <u>not</u> be completely honest and yet remain ethical and good.

One doesn't usually refuse an invitation by telling the caller you don't like him or her when it's easier to say you are busy when actually not. That's because we rationalize a figurative good the little "indiscretion" will serve as opposed to the disproportionate inconvenience, pain, or damage should the truth be known. When your mother asks your opinion of an ugly dress you know she loves, some may shade their response to avoid depriving her of an inconsequential, yet compelling <u>pleasure of the moment</u>—(a morally arguable choice)—with a <u>true</u> opinion couched in an evasive response. We may be a little less than honest to instill motivation. "That's not too bad" when, in fact, it stinks. You've employed honest intent without bludgeoning the person's ardor with the absolute truth. Some circumstances may compel a modification to avoid unreasonable or overly injurious consequences should the truth be known. (*In response to your question, boss: "I'm taking the afternoon off to interview for another job ..."*) Yeah, right!

However, there <u>are</u> circumstances when a higher value or purpose may legitimately usurp what you know or feel is true—a place where outright lies could conceivably serve a higher purpose or a greater value.

International diplomacy often couches the truth in service to a preferred or more rational outcome (national security). Interrogation, defeating a threatened suicide, hostage negotiations, and undercover roles may preempt the truth for the sake of a morally justified and preferred outcome—saving a life or resolving a heinous crime.

A media person may employ ways to get around the absolute truth through conscious omission, off the record agreements, or "No comment" for the sake of preventing panic, violence, premature misperceptions, or being politically correct. *The new-age misnomer: "person of interest" versus suspect.*

You may intensely dislike a colleague or subordinate, but for the sake of professionalism, unit equilibrium, and productivity you employ behaviors and mannerisms that disguise or at least temper your true feelings. So there are situations in which we balance what we know to be true with the merits and applicability of a less than honest action to achieve preferred ethical outcome.

The Problem

The reality of the "street" has many challenges that generate the kind of quandaries managers must deal with in weighing honesty with reality. In the emotional danger zone of human conflict, the harsh reality of frustration, cynicism, and physical harm can generate powerful challenges to honesty in its purest form. Antagonistic clientele and unwieldy episodes make passions flow; unintended words get said, overreactions occur, and wrongs in the heat of conflict happen that can be understood from a human perspective versus what a more official position may require.

Sometimes decisions in reaction to these circumstances are forced upon you without time to sort out what you know to be true. They may seem out of sync with other values having strong and meaningful influence in your life. Immediate and overwhelming challenges can do that, especially when you are managing people you like, and you feel they need and deserve your loyalty. *A long time friend pleads, "Buddy, you've got to help me out of this. No one will understand ..."* It can generate a real battle between wanting to re-work the hierarchy of values in favor of something you are passionately attached to versus the potential harm a (truth) conveyed will do.

When whatever you did or failed to do is revisited by a legitimate authority with the power to exact consequences, consciously omitting or conveniently forgetting something you are obligated to reveal is another dilemma. Or, when we take selective truths from an incident and employ excuses to rework the message more to our benefit. *Yes Sir, I was at the scene, but I was rummaging through the trunk of my car for something when the alleged incident occurred.* "It's one thing not to offer, but to say I didn't know when you did is quite another," according to Edwin Delattre, PhD, Professor of Philosophy, Emeritus, Boston University, and author of the book "Character and Cops." [4]

During testimony at trial, you begin to suspect defense questioning is tricking you with an unrelated issue construed to damage the case to which you are passionately committed. *"Sergeant, have you ever uttered a racial or ethnic slur in the performance of your duties?"* You feel they're pushing the legal envelope, operating outside the rules. How far will your loyalty to a cause or allegiance to a friend propel you into subjugating honesty for the sake of something else? *"No, Your Honor, my informant was not at the scene."* Revealing that he was would seriously threaten the informant's safety as well as continued usefulness in providing what you rationalize to be information of greater importance than the proper adjudication of the issue at hand.

---

4 Edwin Delattre, *Character and Cops, Ethics in Policing,* American Enterprise Institute for Public Policy Research, Washington, D.C., 1989. 36.

Loyalty to your investigation or to another person for what you think is a higher principle or cause than what the law requires will invariably involve a risk far beyond any ill conceived sense of noble self-sacrifice you may feel at the time. Any employee who engages immoral, unethical, or illegal behavior that engulfs other employees usually does so without regard for how it impacts them. However, it often forces uninvolved, observing colleagues into a decision making predicament. *An officer blatantly violates use of force rules in front of peers, forcing them into the quandary of having to decide between two wrongs—the offender and the officer.*

Sometimes a problem employee can be one of your productive employees—*generating numbers their way as opposed to what is required, preferred, and professional. The officer exercising no discretion where warranted for the sake of a statistic.* Managers aware of this imbalance, and do nothing to correct it, only enable and even sanction it through omission, and set themselves up for probable future problems. These are situations that can coerce you into considering consequences that could threaten the continued equilibrium and productivity of the *entire* group or unit. *One employee illicitly obtains answers to a test and passes them on to other employees.* When a problem employee or whistle blower raises an issue you feel threatens the status or survival of something you truly believe in, and you question their motives, what will you do in response to this challenge?

The Answer

As a person of good character, you are prepared to stick to the principles and values that lie deep within your character, and apply them honestly to the situation—above your own self interest. Not revealing what you know by omitting, inventing, or contriving information to achieve a knowingly devious or misleading outcome serves no acceptable or rational purpose. *The offender was not armed when he was mistakenly shot, and there are sirens in the distance and the on-scene officers worry about getting their story straight. They turn what may have been a defendable mistake into a criminal conspiracy by falling victim to those sinister words "all we have to do is stick together."*

To report your daily actions or observation under color of official duty truthfully should be equal to any official review or inquiry. Certainly a court of law serves as a defining parameter for any bottom line. Although reality can sometimes generate special circumstances, whatever you say or do in response to any lawful review of your responsibilities should have <u>no equal, wiggle room, or rationalized higher outcome</u>. This includes any suspicion you have as to the validity of its purpose (politics of the process), and that its origin stems from a devious or less valid venue (*a local activist alleging nonsense for media attention and blatant self interest*). This should never outweigh the basic need for honesty—even when you *feel* an honest response could be misconstrued to serve an ulterior or damaging purpose.

Reporting requirements, either oral or written—regardless of its potential impact on the current issue—is the venue where <u>no other value</u> transcends honesty. Anything which requires reporting, recording, or documentation should reflect the truth as you know it—regardless of its intent, any intervening pressure or feared consequences. It should be your bottom line—the point where there is no higher rationale to legitimize your lapse in revealing what you know as the truth. The line you never cross—<u>regardless of the circumstances</u>.

Your ability to uphold this standard will invariably track back to your relationship with the law, your position, role, and responsibilities.

Our ability to achieve true justice relies on an oath-based means to ensure the truth. At the core of this oath-based process lies our character—the very soul of who we are both to ourselves and others. Regardless of how well intended or justifiable your action was, it is when that action is reviewed or its outcome was not as intended that your bottom line becomes the key to your personal integrity and conscience. One might get away with an omission, revision, or falsehood, but he or she won't escape their conscience. According to the American Enterprise Institute for Public Policy Research, "Silence is not a lie, but it tolerates falsehood, thereby sanctioning it." And conscience comes from knowing what should be done, but choosing or being coerced to do otherwise.

Morality, ethics, virtue, responsibility, duty, righteousness, justice, reason, etc., are the underpinnings of a civilized society. In law enforcement they are the ideals by which we apply ourselves for the good of everyone. Their individual definitions, not withstanding, intertwine to serve as the best direction in which to devote our thoughts and actions.

Law enforcers are not only tasked with enforcing the law, but *upholding* it as well. Law enforcers are the basis of our ability to remain a civilized society. As a nation of laws and a predominantly religious culture, our whole system depends on everyone's acceptance of this standard. The law enforcer's position comes with inherent expectations that make it different from the private sector—namely trust, accountability, and properly executed lawful authority should protect the best interests of everyone. Polls show police enjoy a high level of trust. It could be higher if not for the few instances where honesty gets subjugated for misguided lesser values—whether it's friendship, loyalty, self preservation, fear or other influences.

The capability of law enforcement agencies to effectively deal with their own deficiencies is hugely important to the overall perception of the public's trust in your efforts. When officers lie or cover up, or allow continued malfeasance, it undermines the public's trust in the organization, lessens their propensity to cooperate, and severely limits the organization's purpose. It becomes the basis for a self defeating prophecy.

Public service stems from the law. In a court of law, 'under oath' is the last bastion of our belief in justice and our system. It is important to remember when deciding what to do—which value to prioritize when faced with an emotion laden conflict or challenge.

The Challenge:

It is important to understand and be prepared to accept whatever consequences may result when challenged under these conditions. Taking an oath to reveal what you know is certainly one of those times. To lie or mislead under oath in a legally recognized proceeding is not only a crime, but in direct defiance of one's own sworn commitment to honestly carry out one's duty. It was a commitment made voluntarily from what should be the depth of your heart and character. **It should be the defining moment of your bottom line.**

So, yes, honesty is the best policy. It is important to determine your bottom line with regard to this value—<u>before</u> you inadvertently pass it for the sake of anything else—especially misguided loyalty and/or misunderstood friendship.

CHAPTER 9

Loyalty

It's like fire. It can warm you against the elements or burn you if you're not careful.

A very popular and productive officer is stopping and ticketing "certain" motorists for minor offenses in hopes of discovering some form of more serious criminality. He has often bragged that "these people" are where it's "happening" in terms of discovering contraband. He regularly searches without justification or consent. His escapades generate amusement and war stories from colleagues. Some comment if they had to do anything dangerous (go through a door), they would like to have him by their side. They seem in awe of his aggressiveness and bravado. The officer is under investigation for what a local activist claims is a pattern of ethnic and racial profiling by the department. Internal Affairs is seeking any knowledge you may have concerning his activities.

**

A boss you like, who mentored and supported you throughout your career and selected you for your supervisory position, is facing what you believe are unfair accusations from a disgruntled whistle blower. He or she is alleging pervasive sexual harassment throughout the department. You are scheduled to appear before an outside agency charged with investigating these allegations. Although you observed the boss exceed propriety on occasion, you feel an urge to protect and defend. You wonder if there is something that can be done to minimize or counter the whistle blower's claim, which may serve a more important purpose (continued equilibrium of something to which you are passionately attached) than what this one person has to say.

"One for all and all for one," is a cute little phrase from Alexander Dumas's classic, *The Three Musketeers*. It captures an underlying theme many feel obligated to fulfill in order to protect each other against all challenges, and sometimes just to remain accepted within a group. In law enforcement it's often coined in the phrase "each has the other's back." Oh, if it were only that simple.

Like the battered wife who suddenly jumps to her husband's defense when he is arrested for abusing her, sometimes loyalty can override more rational and appropriate actions during times of chaos and controversy.

The elements of loyalty are easiest to fulfill when the controversy being tested involves good intentions or excusable mistakes. However, **this chapter deals more with loyalty getting hijacked by irresponsibility or purposeful wrong, or when a friend's conduct, so admirable in the past, suddenly violates an ideal that also has your loyalty.**

What is loyalty, really?

It is a commitment you bestow on someone or something in the form of sincere belief, moral support, extended effort, and especially the benefit of any doubt in favor of the recipient during times of controversy. To be loyal is to fulfill your part of what are usually in-formal social bargains.[5] It is also a personal choice.

We choose to whom or whatever we will be loyal, and rank them ac-cording to our choice of priority. *I will be more loyal to my children than to others. I will be more loyal to my agency than another should they be in conflict.* They are choices one makes that come with no definitive obligation other than what is too often expected by others. However, when one swears an oath, then "choice" becomes more definitive, obligatory, and steadfast.

The dictionary defines loyalty as steadfast in allegiance as to one's homeland, and faithful as to a person, ideal, cause, or duty. *The word 'steadfast' is somewhat problematic in that it implies 'fixed' or 'unchanging,' which is part of the dilemma when applied to another person or group involved in a wrong.* Synonyms include fidelity, allegiance, duty, faithfulness, trustworthiness, and devotion.

Loyalty lies at the root of reliability, a strong ingredient for cohesive-ness, trustworthiness, and group equilibrium. It is an important ele-ment in any friendship. It is a value that applies across a wide spec-trum of recipients in varying degrees of intensity and level of com-mitment (tiered loyalty), i.e., family, friends, colleagues, acquain-tances, principles, ideals, and organizations.

Loyalty is most profound in those organizations or jobs that promote cohesiveness, team building, elitism, or uniqueness. Law enforcement agencies are a prime example—you take an oath to commit to certain ideals and the law, and depend greatly on peers and the organization for support and safety in situations that can be both emotionally and physically traumatic. It is a career where the pull and power of peer

---

5 Eric Felton, *Loyalty, the Vexing Virtue,* (New York. Simon & Shuster, 2011). 34

relationships can override the more distant and sometimes abstract draw of purpose and principles. *When you're in a tight situation on the street, the survival or safety of your partner can become more of a concern than the law or the rules and regulations that apply to it. The soldier who charges the machine gun nest does so more out of loyalty to his comrades than any attachment to a principle of winning the battle or supporting a cause.* However, as a manager much of your job will require you to think of the law and the principles that underlie and sanction the organization and its mission—regardless of the circumstances.

Although usually demonstrated by sustained countenance and patronage over time, one's loyalty is most often judged by how one reacts to a challenge impacting the recipient of his or her loyal focus.

When standing before an invading foreign army one would understandably place loyalty above honesty in defense of his or her peers when their personal safety is at stake. Coincidentally, our federalist form of government induces similar suspicion in those who view "outside" interests or intervention in a similar manner—as a threat or intruder. Municipalities do not like being meddled with by the state, and both have reservations about any federal level intrusions. There are over 17,000 law enforcement agencies in this country, each imbued with a sense of self-rule, independent thought, and a natural tendency to maintain and safeguard their respective jurisdiction. It is the very nature of our political being.

There is often a distrusting nature and defensive posture when colleagues are investigated by another agency and/or even by their own internal processes. In police work it is often called "the blue wall,"— an "us versus them" orientation, which evolves from this kind of innate mistrust, bureaucratic myopia, and what is too often a misguided and parochial view of loyalty.

The inclination to passionately defend what or who one is loyal to contains pitfalls for managers, especially when the recipient of such loyalty is purposely or recklessly wrong and your knowledge could be harmful. (*In the example at the beginning of this chapter, you once witnessed the boss grope an employee, and the victim has testified that you witnessed the incident*). It can become a real paradox for the unprepared manager.

The crucible erupts when you feel a need to influence or impede the lawful source attempting to resolve an issue in favor of someone or something to which you are loyal. Or, those in need of your loyalty blatantly seek to use your loyalty to mislead or impede the lawful source of their challenge.

Therefore, when the pull of this value draws you into a questionable circumstance, it becomes necessary to reassess the merits of your belief in this value. You must consider how it can remain a value in its truest sense and not become something else.

The Dilemma

There's an old adage in police work that goes, "If you're not in trouble, you're <u>not</u> doing your job." It is a cynical view that sums up the volatility and ambiguity that anyone actively engaged in resolving human conflict can encounter. It could be overlooking minor (sometimes serious) transgressions of a valuable informant, or deciding to ignore certain factors in a domestic dispute for a possible peaceful resolution, etc. They are any one of a number of discretionary judgments made each shift that can bite you later on. What you thought were rational decisions, you may later feel will be perceived differently by others—*those on the "street" that require quick and sometimes less than desired outcomes versus what some may see from the more insulated and sanctimonious analytical positions of higher rank and review staff.* This perceived reality is what can feed the steadfastness of this value some may feel obligated to fulfill, regardless of the circumstances or consequences.

That's because …

Loyalty can be a <u>very</u> subjective value. *Yes, it is one of choice, but choosing is often heavily influenced by the expectations of others.* There are some who measure loyalty by length of service without any issues. Others may have a myopic or selfish sense of ownership—a "with me or against me" kind of stance. The recipient of your loyalty may expect <u>you</u> to do whatever <u>they</u> feel loyalty is, regardless of the circumstances or the consequences—right or wrong. Some may feel you should be willing to risk *whatever* it takes to accommodate <u>their</u> agenda (*even lie if necessary*) in order to maintain their trust in you. It is amazing how some managers consider <u>any</u> questioning of their wishes, or fraternizing with people or other agencies outside <u>their</u> favor as disloyal.

If it isn't the draw of loyalty that lures one into deviousness, then it's probably the fear of being considered <u>disloyal</u> or labeled "a rat" that can influence one in times of controversy and challenge. The fear and <u>stigma</u> of being considered <u>dis</u>loyal can heavily influence one's thinking during times of controversy and prompt unanticipated and surprising reactions. Betrayal is the antithesis of loyalty and a serious negative in our society and culture. Some will risk severe consequences in the name of loyalty to avoid being labeled disloyal, or accrue the even more despicable title of 'rat.'

An aversion to confront unethical or illegal acts and reveal wrongs for the sake of a more distant ideal like ethics, morality, mission, or *purpose* is a powerful constraint that requires great courage and commitment to overcome. *Studies have shown that even the most stringent codes for honesty and loyalty to high ideals, as required in our prestigious military academies, can fall victim to the lure of loyalty to peers and colleagues for less valid reasons. The fear of disloyalty's consequences—a perceived distrust and loss of respect from peers, probable ostracism, and retaliation—can trump the fear of discovery and possible dismissal for failing to uphold a more distant ideal or code.*

However, one of the reasons loyalty is so well regarded is that the <u>perception</u> of betrayal is fairly commonplace. There is a 17th century English adage that says, "In time of prosperity friends will be plenty / In time of adversity not one among twenty."[6] It is common because—like loyalty—betrayal is the standard too often determined by the beholder (reason for crucible). *Most fail to consider the real rat in every pickle. Yes, it's probable one will be labeled a rat for failing to uphold another's expectation of doing whatever is necessary to protect them from disclosure. However, the <u>real</u> rat is the one who created the issue in the first place and now expects another to sacrifice his or her integrity for the sake of the instigator's bad judgment.*

A loyalty test for managers usually involves a conflict between a sense of commitment to an individual, group, or process one believes in and relies on, and duties and responsibilities of the oath he or she has sworn to fulfill, which now threatens that balance. It can push years of commitment and loyalty up to one number on the craps table. In other words, regardless of how loyal you've been over the years, the test you are facing becomes the watershed that trumps all prior efforts to fulfill this value. You may owe <u>your</u> position to the subject of the controversy, and now you are faced with having to reveal, report, or testify to something that could damage his or her career and livelihood by honorably fulfilling the duties and responsibilities you've sworn to uphold.

You *want* to believe your loyalty recipient's claims of ignorance or innocence, but instinct tells you otherwise. This is where the benefit of doubt plays a role, but be careful of the action you take in defer-

6 Ibid., 151

ence to this position. It is important to know the difference between what you *want* to be true and what you actually know to be true. The benefit of doubt means not concluding one way or the other. It's okay—even laudatory—to defend the integrity of the other as you <u>know it</u>, without fabricating or embellishing whatever it is <u>you want to be true.</u>

An officer makes a reckless mistake, and it results in a fatality or other serious consequence. Where will your loyalty take you? Will it be to the reckless officer at the expense of the organization's reputation for not upholding the law? If so, then why? Someone may do something wrong in defense of the organization. Does your loyalty to the organization now automatically transfer to the wrongdoer? *A seasoned manager shreds a document important to an outside investigative effort he felt would besmirch the organization's reputation.* To what extent will you compromise your principles or cross what should have been your bottom line for the sake of this value?

When a friend or recipient of your loyalty tells you one thing, but facts and circumstances say another, then anything said or done in defense of that person must be carefully gauged. *The officer tells you his firearm discharged by mistake when he shot an unarmed suspect, versus valid witnesses stating they heard the officer say to the victim seconds before the shot, "Here, see how this feels you little #%&."* The offender may be evil and despicable, but you'll find the issue of loyalty lies not between the officer and the offender, or what he or she did, but what the officer is sworn to do and your obligation to conduct yourself within the same context.

What happens when equal values collide?

This happens when loyalty to someone or thing challenges your responsibility to another. When loyalty to the law, truth, and duty—what you have *sworn* to uphold—threatens your devotion to family, friends, the organization, or another important ideal or circumstance, etc. As an example, risking the organization's reputation and/or your family's welfare (if you are found out and lose your job or go to jail) to protect a fellow officer or even a valued informant with any kind of deception during an official inquiry or court challenge. It could be a dispute between a subordinate or a group to which you wish to remain loyal and the employer to whom you are equally committed. Having a good sense of what and who you *should be* (bottom line) loyal to is important at times like this—to be on the right side for the right reasons. In the case of divided loyalties, to whom or what will your deference lie?

Time for Questions

What is <u>your</u> understanding of loyalty? Are you engaging in actions you believe the recipient (or others) expect, or what *you* believe the value to be? Is your interpretation supporting someone in times of need, extending doubt, and/or sticking by the recipient <u>right or wrong</u>? What happens when the recipient is accused of something you suspect or know to be true? Yes, you both may have overcome many challenges together, and your entire career could be embedded in that person's respect and affinity for you. It may be he or she took a risk to select or defend you—and weathered a controversy on your behalf. How far will your sense of loyalty drive you to defend the person involved in a wrong to repay a debt? Do you feel compelled to do something that you also feel is in conflict with what you are sworn to do?

What is your stake in the issue? Are you truly part of the resolution or just a bystander feeling an urge to inject yourself into the middle of something for the sake of friendship or loyalty?

Is it possible to be both honest and loyal—even if honesty is in defiance of someone's expectations? For example speaking up, being truthful when others are not? In other words, sometimes playing the messenger of bad tidings or opposing views <u>for the recipient's benefit</u> is a more valid stance. *You've heard the boss refer to female officers in derogatory terms. Did you laugh at the remarks, ignore them, or caution the boss of their potential negative ramifications?*

If you engage a cover-up for the sake of one or a few and get caught, how will the revelation adversely impact the reputation of other non-involved officers and the longer term benefit of public trust? How does the immediate test play out against the potential welfare or survival of other things you should be loyal to?

Loyalty should be reciprocal in its truest form. In other words, you are loyal to another because you both share similar values and practice what *you* believe to be right. You perceive him or her to be honest, conducting themselves in line with <u>proper</u> values and expectations, and whatever is at issue came from honest intent or an excusable mistake (*a split second decision or honest belief*).

Be careful that whatever mistakes or deficiencies you are willing to overlook or forgive do not unduly influence your sense of right and wrong. Does the difficulty of your job really excuse excessive or less than normal performance based on what may be a cynical misperception or bad attitude? (*The citizen doesn't know what I'm up against; they don't see all the evil I do.*) In other words, is there <u>any</u> legitimate excuse for failing to perform as required or not telling the truth?

What are the elements necessary to fulfill <u>your</u> perception of this value? Here is where it can burn you. It now becomes a matter of knowing what *you* believe are the proper elements of this value. It is this kind of self reflection that strikes at the very heart of this bottom line issue. A good place to begin is with …

What Loyalty is NOT

Efforts bestowed to another out of fear or coercion aren't loyal, but more like subjugation and domination, even cowardice.

Too often loyalty can become more servile and selfish than faithful and honest, like those who extend the benefit of doubt beyond reason—to blind servitude. These people are not loyal, but more like facilitators and enablers. It may fit the recipient's perception of loyalty, but denies the loyalist the true meaning of the word.

It should never be considered obligatory—especially if the recipient is purposely wrong. It should not be reciprocal on its face just because it's loyalty. One may demand it, but should not expect it if it is a purposeful wrong or inadequacy that drives the quandary.

It should not be compensatory either, especially when you further another's position absent the qualities to hold it. The landscape is littered with examples of people being placed beyond their capacity for loyalty's sake. Rewarding allegiance or friendship by elevating the stalwart to some position within your power is not loyalty—it is nepotism.

Loyalty should be broad based and open to question. Blind loyalty can be trouble. It should never be the "fall on the sword" kind of commitment, where you sacrifice your values, principles and/or reputation. That is not loyalty—it is stupidity.

To commit a wrong in the name of loyalty for the sake of the agency, ideal, or whomever is—in reality—disloyal. *The revelation of the previously mentioned manager shredding the document did much damage to the reputation of the agency and created a more sinister (inculpatory) spin for the challenge he was hoping to nullify.*

There may be situations where colleagues get corralled into being part of the problem. In other words other employees—either directly or indirectly—are suddenly part of a "blue wall" or cover-up. Is it really loyalty to join the coterie and look the other way, or is it joining a conspiracy and committing a crime?

Is the fear of being perceived as disloyal and being ostracized or socially isolated driving your actions? Then it's no longer loyalty—it is now cowardice in terms of knowing what should be done, but you don't because of fear or coercion.

Loyalty is <u>not</u> something one should bestow unconditionally. It must be assumed the recipient lives up to the basic framework *you* feel deserves your loyalty. *If you play by the rules, so should the recipient.*

Any employee committing an intentional or irresponsible wrong should fall outside the parameters of what loyalty deserves. The wrongful employee is the one who is disloyal. He or she is the one who intentionally or recklessly puts others needlessly at risk, thereby undermining the bottom line tenet of "One for all and all for one." The officer who wantonly beats a victim, regardless of how despicable the person is, does so without regard for the quandary and consequences his or her actions pose for fellow officers. When law enforcement personnel violate their oath, they not only fail the true test of loyalty, but fail themselves as people of character, too.

<u>Revisiting Oaths:</u>

It's time to revisit and familiarize yourself with what loyalty in the workplace *should be,* by reviewing it in the context of your sworn commitment. In spite of the trouble that faces the recipient of your loyalty focus, what is the true essence of this value, and how should it be applied to the issue at hand? It is an essential part for knowing your bottom line <u>when</u> you need to know it—<u>before</u> it gets overwhelmed by unexpected circumstances.

In law enforcement you have many areas of routine loyalty focus—another person (your partner), the group to which you belong, the organization as a whole, and many other associations with which you are involved. However, if any of these entities should come into conflict, where will your highest preference lie? Will it be to the partner who backs you up, the organization that pays your salary, etc., regardless of the circumstances? *It is important to remember that you have not sworn an oath to those entities.* Or will it be the principles and authority upon which it is all sanctioned to exist? It will be your choice.

In the law enforcement realm, there are two pledges you will make that should transcend everything and anything you may have previously sworn to.

(1) *Will the graduates please stand, raise their right hand, and repeat after me, "I solemnly swear to defend the Constitution of the United States ..." etc., etc.*

(2) *Raise your right hand and repeat after me, "Do you swear to tell the truth, the whole truth, and nothing but the truth, so help you God?"*

Where will the oath of office and swearing yourself to reveal the absolute truth in a court of law fit in relation to all other commitments—sworn or otherwise, i.e., the Pledge of Allegiance, Scout's Honor, military duty, local clubs and organizations, and other promises based on long standing associations accumulated along the way?

Oaths of Office and Courtroom Testimony

Have you ever wondered about the significance of raising one's hand to swear an oath or make a pledge? As it turns out, it has a long, yet uncertain cultural and legal history that lends a physical gesture to a ritual, which helps accentuate what should be a meaningful and al-most spiritual commitment one is making to whatever is being sworn. It often joins with pomp and circumstance to intensify and strengthen the solemnity necessary for added emphasis and meaning. However, the essence of any oath goes far beyond symbols and words, and there lies the crux of this very important part of a public servant's professional persona.

Unfortunately, oaths administered to law enforcers too frequently are a perfunctory administrative exercise seldom repeated or revisited during the tenure of their employment. It is often a quick one-time shot (*Raise your right hand and repeat after me*) with little indoctrination and lesser follow up. This, as opposed to a physician's commitment (sometimes signed) to medical ethics via the Hippocratic Oath. While it seems to be under constant debate and change, the oath remains a solid subject of medical training and a guide for doctors to consider in pursuit of their profession.

By raising one's right hand and placing it on a bible, over your heart or a document, one is communicating in both words *and* gesture what is supposed to be a *wholehearted* intent to live up to whatever is being sworn. It is more than a promise. It should underscore a conscious realization that this newly sworn commitment will invariably chal-lenge other promises made along the way. An oath should be at the forefront of everything we do in public service, and redefine the con-cept of loyalty.

When one stands at the altar of marriage and swears to love, hold and cherish another, they are officially and publically relegating all other accumulated associa-tions and friendships to a lesser role in their life. It is a conscious and voluntary choice one makes, which pushes loyalty to others down a notch to make way for loyalty to one (One of the reasons so many are invited to witness the event). When one's friends don't like the betrothed, some brides and grooms may refrain from committing to the marriage. However, once one says "I do," then the message to others should be pretty clear as to where loyalty will lie in regard to any future clash between friends, family, and the newly proclaimed husband and wife. The same should apply to the role that swearing to uphold the law as a law enforcer takes with all others—including friends and relatives.

Oaths affirm and convey what should be a conscious <u>conviction</u> to commit one's self in both belief and intent to fulfill that which you're swearing to uphold. *It should be a transforming experience.* The depth of your personal conviction will be the key to its actual fulfillment. It should sit at the core of your character and become the force of reasoning, which applies to all situations that test the value of loyalty. An oath should create a strong sense of obligation, which should rework your understanding of loyalty and where it legitimately lies in the hierarchy of all recipients and other values.

However, one can swear to all he or she wants, but like a "bottom line," it isn't until your commitment gets <u>tested</u> that the true meaning of this rite comes to the fore. All the hand raising, pomp and circumstance, means little in comparison to what has to <u>be</u> in terms of <u>how you *actually* think and feel</u>.

"I, (name), <u>so solemnly</u> swear (or affirm) that I will support and defend the Constitution of the United States against all enemies, foreign and domestic; that I will bear true faith and allegiance to the same; that I take this obligation freely, without any mental reservation or purpose of evasion, and I will well and faithfully discharge the duties of the office on which I am about to enter. So help me God." U.S. Code, 5 USC: 3331 (delineates the Oath of Office and the Constitution)

The federal pledge is clear that the United States Constitution is the ultimate and singular recipient of one's sworn loyalty, which includes all laws and regulations throughout its legal venues and lifespan. There are no references to any person, department or community.

Most state and local oaths revolve around the U.S. Constitution or the derivative laws of the state therein. Through an oath one is swearing his or her true faith and allegiance (loyalty) to principles of law that transcend the demands of everyday relationships and dilemmas. You are not just swearing to a document that creates the framework and authority of our government as we know it, but more importantly, to a complex of ideals in its Bill of Rights that impacts everything one does as a law enforcer. So, it is a big deal and deserves much more effort to educate and understand than just, "repeat after me ..."

The reason the oath of office and courtroom pledge trump other promises made along the way has a lot to do with the concept of public trust.

When a citizen pins on a badge and recites an oath of office, they are voluntarily swearing to bear the public trust.[7] Public trust lies at the core of our ability to perform effectively. It is key to the stability and survival of our communities and nation. We are a nation of laws. From common to constitutional, they are the foundation for ensuring the safety, dignity, and welfare of all citizens. The U.S. Constitution is the source of all laws and propriety throughout our nation—from the office of the Presidency down to each state, municipality, and individual. As the source of all law, the United States Constitution structures government to ensure the basic rights of citizens through fairness, equality, restraint of power, and sensitivity to civil rights.

From this foundation grows the process of lawful authority, the means to ensure the intent and purpose of our governing remains intact and strong. This includes not only the authority of a law en-

---

7   Edwin J. Delattre. Character and Cops, Ethics in Policing (Washington, D.C., American Enterprise Institute for Public Policy Research. 1989) 32

forcer, but also those with oversight responsibility to ensure the propriety of those with powers over others. Oversight exists for the protection of <u>everyone</u> and acts as the check that balances our sense of democracy. Every official, from the President, the judiciary, the high school principal and the law enforcer, can be held accountable and prosecuted. It is a powerful undercurrent to everything we do as members of this society. It is a covenant that most—thankfully—accept and strive to fulfill.

An oath helps bolster every citizen's faith that those employed in the public sector will uphold the ideals they have sworn themselves to do. The act of swearing an oath should be meaningful enough to transform the person from what they were to the public servant they now become. It should represent a solid foundation of indoctrination meaningful enough to carry one through the years after the impact of the ceremony has long faded, and the reality of experience pummels their resolve. It's important to fully understand and accept where the oath should side with regard to whatever temptation or conflict there is to sway you otherwise. It lies at the heart of most controversies that become crucibles.

One of the most compelling tests for sorting and prioritizing loyalty to principle and the law occurred in March of 2004. FBI Director Robert Mueller faced President George Bush over the legality of a highly sensitive and very controversial counter terrorist surveillance program aimed at further securing the country against terror. Director Mueller along with Acting Attorney General James Comey were both prepared to tender their resignations over certain aspects of the program Mueller felt was illegal to operate. Whereas the administration viewed the surveillance program as a necessity for the nation's security, Mueller felt just the opposite. The nation's security rested with its primacy of law. As he said in a speech he

gave later, "The rule of law, civil liberties, and civil rights—these are not bounda-
ries. They are what make all of us stronger and safer ..." [8]

Speaking of which, the Attorneys General (AG) of the United States
is a good example for this kind of dilemma. He or she must balance
between the oath of office and protecting the person (President) who
selected him or her for the job. The AG owes a debt of gratitude and
degree of deference, which can test the sense of loyalty right to its
core. It is a valid quandary up until he or she places one hand on the
bible, raises their right hand, and so <u>solemnly</u> swears. It will certainly
factor heavily into the source of courage anyone has to muster during
times of extreme pressure, stress, and quandary. Anyone mentoring,
favoring, or selecting you for promotion must expect this, as well.

**Where does the oath you take to bear the public trust sit in your
repertoire of values and principles? The commitment to and
attendant value of loyalty should be elevated far beyond the
mere formality of repeating words.**

In cases of outright support to others regardless of the circumstances
and consequences as with your children and family, the moral question becomes what this support will entail? Will it mean straying from
permissible help to unethical or illegal obstruction and abetting? Two
noteworthy examples for testing familial (sibling) loyalty stem from
serial bomber Ted Kaczynski and mob murderer Whitey Bulger.
Both of these men murdered innocent people. Both had law abiding
brothers. One helped authorities bring his brother to justice
(Kaczynski); the other (Bulger) did not. One was loyal to principle,
the other to a person. Which brother was more "right?" Which took
more courage? Which should garner more respect?

---

8 Garrett M. Graff, *The Threat Matrix: The FBI At War In The Age Of
  Global Terror.* (New York, Little Brown and Company, 2011)
  497–491

A crucible may require you to withstand the possibility of being thought of by the recipient and others as disloyal in the short term, before the true nature of your loyalty can be known. That's because loyalty has everything to do with truth and honesty and nothing with ignoring or covering up inadequacies or indiscretions. Loyalty is best fulfilled when the loyalist provides the recipient with the kind of advice and counsel that serves the recipient's long term best interest without deception. Loyalty should include a well balanced source of input bearing both good and bad news. (Telling a friend he or she drinks too much and advising appropriate remedies versus ignoring it or offering another drink).

Loyalty isn't ignoring, facilitating, abetting, or covering up a deficiency or wrong. It has to do with confronting it and working to correct or alleviate it sooner rather than later—to provide whomever what they should be hearing and not what you think they want to hear, or avoiding what they don't want to hear. It is being reliable, faithful and supportive for the "best interests" of the recipient that doesn't compromise your integrity, sense of right and wrong, and the oath you've sworn . It's when you can face the group and say, "We screwed up and now is not the time to make it worse. We must accept responsibility, endure the consequences, and move on."

When used improperly (*like blindly following the party line*)—is it really loyalty or a lesser value like greed, pandering, or self aggrandizement? Remember, loyalty can still be fulfilled without having to prove your level of commitment through a wrongful or misleading act.

In every challenge it is important to focus on the "origins" of the issue under review. Are they innocent, well intended in a moral and legal sense versus a reckless, irresponsible or conscious wrong? When asked, directed, or influenced to do something not true to the facts as you know them, don't let the immediacy and intensity of the situation or another's expectations cloud your thoughts. Keep in mind what you have sworn to do for the good of the larger aspects of your life and that of the organization. *A fellow officer is obviously at fault in a serious car accident off duty. You smell alcohol on his breath, and it is normal procedure to have the driver take a breathalyzer test. But you do not.* If you think loyalty is driving your urge to ignore or cover up, it is not. It's more like a conspiracy, and may deprive loyalty of its greatest value—to the organization as a whole and its responsible employees, while bearing the public trust. *Besides, where was everyone's loyalty when the person was evolving into that kind of behavior?*

One can still carry out his or her duties and yet stand by the accused recipient of your loyalty during post incident reviews and adjudication. If you feel that strongly about the recipient, you can help in any legally acceptable way to fulfill your sense of loyalty. A nationally prominent coach of college basketball continued his loyalty to a couple of star players who failed their team by engaging in off-court criminal activity. He cooperated truthfully with authorities, which undoubtedly added to the negativity of their consequences, yet stood by the players throughout their disciplinary ordeal. He remained loyal to them in their plight <u>apart</u> from their wrongdoing, yet stayed true to the law and spirit of proper sportsmanship and leadership responsibilities.

The oath of office should be revisited on occasion. There is nothing wrong with reaffirming, even recommitting to the oath of office when promoted up the chain of command. Each promotion is the perfect time to do this, with added caveats of good management practices, i.e., to be fair, truthful, and accountable for my actions, etc.

The linchpin to all values is the principle of honesty—to you and to all others. While there are some situations where honesty can be subjugated for a higher moral purpose, it's when the issue challenges one's oath to the law in any legal venue that honesty should prevail without question. <u>It's the bottom line not crossed—regardless of the consequences</u>.

The most loyal are those who stay true to oaths they have taken, who value honesty in the highest realm, and take responsibility for their actions. They expect the same from others, and face and endure the consequences—whatever they may be.

CHAPTER 10

Friendship

There's an old saying that goes, "With my enemies I can deal, God help me with my friends and family." It brings home the depth of emotion, frustration and mystique that can attach itself to this area of social interaction—a relationship with another that has special meaning and preference.

It was a difficult arrest. The offender refused to be handcuffed. The struggle involved a number of officers wrestling the offender to the ground. Some punches were exchanged, and he was finally subdued and cuffed. When repositioned upright, the offender spit at an officer and called him a derogatory name. The officer, a personal friend, someone you've known most of your life, called the offender a racial slur and tried to punch him in the face with a glancing blow off the guy's shoulder. You and other officers intervened, pulling your friend back. You told your friend to cool off and directed him away from the offender. You verbally reprimanded your friend and told him you never wanted to see anything like that again. He agreed, apologized, expressed remorse, and said he understood your position.

The next day the Chief stops you in the hallway and says, "I understand there was a beef yesterday with an arrest. Is there anything I should know?" You sense his request is for any potential problems that could emanate from the incident.

You respond with sufficient information regarding the difficulty in securing the offender, but don't mention the actions of your friend.

A while later it's a different story. You are being asked by a lawful source taking notes and/or recording your response to "Did you see Officer X (your friend) strike and call the accused a racially derisive name <u>after</u> he was secured?" You suspect that other officers have denied seeing or hearing anything. <u>Suddenly, it is crucible time</u>.

Most friendships revolve around shared experiences of a social nature. It could be a work setting, helping each other with projects, social gatherings, and recreational activities, etc. However, those activities are vastly different than the kind being addressed in this chapter.

This chapter addresses the test of friendship that comes with the challenge faced by one that intensifies a need for questionable or high risk tangible support from another.

What is a friend, really?

Noted author and professor, James Q. Wilson, in his book "The Moral Sense," asserts that one's basic sense for friendship is <u>reciprocity</u>—a belief that what I feel for a friend, the friend will respond in kind. It is a strong human bond people rank very high in their cache of life's personal preferences.

Time, proximity, common interest, and shared experiences also add to the mix. A 'good' person normally looks for similar qualities in another, as will the less inclined likely gravitate otherwise. (*Birds of a feather flock together*). It is a value that provides social warmth, balance, a sense of security, and a degree of intimacy one consciously keeps from others. Trust is an inherent part of this value. Friendship is certainly a strong component in a successful marriage. It can also involve a sacred trust or special need as in being named best man, matron of honor, estate executor, etc.

Many variables comprise a hierarchy that sorts how one friend fits into all other relationships. For example, some may value looks, personality, social status, physical prowess, etc., in ranking one relationship above another. Others may consider a friend based on a few common interests, time spent together, a shared work endeavor, being a neighbor, an occasional social engagement, or—for some in today's cyberspace environment—just communicating through mediums where they have never met face to face.

The intensity of a shared experience can create a unique bond, too. You may not be particularly friendly with the other person, but the bond that develops from a shared significant experience (combat, survival, or what you both do for a living all of which require a high degree of cohesiveness and camaraderie) can create a friendly connection, too, even though you seldom interact with each other. Interpretations of what constitutes a friend can be as varied as the people creating the friendships.

However …

Bottom line: Friends are mostly those who reciprocate with the more intangible forms of sincere concern, empathy, understanding, and great feeling. They truly care about your health and welfare above that of others. They are those for whom you feel the same, and are willing to help to an extent that strikes at the very heart of the concept of a bottom line. A true friend is someone you know would go to great lengths to protect, defend, and help you in time of need, but whom you would <u>not</u> want to put at undue risk by committing a wrong on your behalf.

Loyalty can play a role when a colleague stands accused of something, but friendship makes it a real dilemma if you know or suspect the basis of accusations.

When you observe, learn, or suspect a subordinate friend of doing something wrong, and it comes under scrutiny by an official concern that requires your input, thus begins a challenge to both the reputation and possible career survival of a friend, and the role you'll have to play in its resolution. It is where truth, honesty, and responsibility can become muddled by the emotional influences of loyalty and friendship. It poses a threat to the equilibrium of this special relationship with another.

It will never be a question of helping a friend in need, but the <u>extent</u> and <u>kind</u> of help one provides that will be the basis of this issue.

How do <u>you</u> define a friend? A good start would be with your own perception of what friendship should NOT be.

What Friendship is NOT

Friendship should never be a bond that would require you to commit a wrong to maintain. *"You've got to tell my spouse I was with you <u>all</u> of last night."* Your *friend* is asking you to lie with no higher moral purpose except to avoid an unpleasant consequence of <u>their own</u> making, which now has enveloped you. This person is using the value of your friendship to draw you into doing something a <u>true</u> friend would not have asked you to do.

Any effort to embroil a friend in any kind of wrong doing should not be considered within the realm of this value. To encumber or obligate the other is not what real friendship is about. It becomes something else—a means to use another for your own illicit benefit.

Anything done to abet, enable, or compound a problem of another like ignoring addiction, domestic abuse, malfeasance, improper bias, etc., will never be in the best interest of a friend. While it may seem easier to avoid the immediate (short term) unpleasantness of doing otherwise, don't neglect your friend's best interest.

Thinking through Friendship

Ancient Greek philosopher Aristotle pondered this value centuries ago. However, his analysis remains timely and applicable in today's world. He reasoned three kinds of friendship:

There are the friends we have for pleasure, who entertain us. We enjoy their comradeship, but may not share their views or propensity to behave outside the norm *(a fishing or poker playing buddy, someone to share feelings with, a fellow team member, or a party person whom you like, yet do not necessarily respect or admire)*. They are friends mostly for our amusement or self directed needs.

The second kind has to do with the usefulness of an association *(colleagues, people with influence or power, who can fulfill or further your social, economic, and/or political aims)*. Again, while we may consider them friends in a conventional sense, these are basically relationships we engage in to reap some kind of personal benefit or self aggrandizement.

Aristotle's third and most preferable friendship derives from mutual admiration (friendship in virtue). Mutual admiration usually stems from both believing and upholding similar moral standards and expectations. You *really* like and admire this friendship from a morally based perspective.

The first two kinds of friendships are more self serving and tenuous versus the more *other directed* virtuous kind of relationship. In other words, friendship in its truest (most virtuous) form would never include a selfish, malicious or devious bent. Whatever is done to or for the true friend will be in his or her best interest. Each, out of mutual respect and admiration, has the other's best interest at heart.

Unfortunately, it is the interpretation of another's best interest that can become muddled in situations that drive a crucible. What will truly be in the *best interest* of a friend? In other words, one may think the other's best interest would be to avoid or subvert the immediate challenge or threat as opposed to what may be a more preferable longer term solution. Do you feel compelled to massage the truth to accommodate what you believe *has* to be done to maintain what you think is a close friendship? *If I can help the friend through this initial phase of wrongdoing by omitting or changing the truth, it may derail further interest or action with regard to the matter.* Does the value of this friendship truly justify your urge to rank it above your sworn obligation to be honest? And, does it put at risk a longer term—more preferable—outcome (facing and resolving the issue now versus the risk of enlarging consequences or lingering suspicion of an unresolved wrong that has now ensnared you)?

Another's best interest would normally involve anything ethical or moral that helps regain, retain, or sustain their integrity and sense of well being, thereby helping to protect him or her from greater negative consequences by conspiring otherwise. *The officer was wrong to fire his weapon off duty during a drunken escapade. Is it better to take immediate disciplinary action now—at a conceivably minor stage—versus the risk of creating another more serious wrong with greater consequences?*

It must be understood that all categories of friends, however we define them, are changing as time goes on. Friendships evolve, intensify, and subside as we engage the normal course of living in our modern and mobile society. Even your closest friendship with another may be usurped by an intervening marriage, career move, or the challenge of a crucible.

There was a Chief who lived in a small town and close knit neighborhood. He enjoyed a bevy of friends from around the state who provided an incredible social life and professional esteem—until he lost his job over a political controversy. People whom he thought he knew and considered friends of long standing suddenly turned their backs with no explanation and left him with little of what he once had. It became the greatest anguish of his career—and challenged his belief in the whole concept of friendship.

However, there are positive situations that can change the nature of a friendship rather quickly and substantially, too. When one friend is promoted to a position over another is one such situation. Actually, being promoted reworks the juxtaposition of all relationships. You now have a common interest and shared experiences with others you did not have before. As one rises in the organization, the same concepts that comprise friendship and loyalty enlarge to others who will also depend on you for the leadership and commitment they need to fulfill their goals and expectations. To engage in any kind of activity that risks your responsibility to many for the sake a few is not what friendship should be about.

Superiors you previously related to in more constrained or deferential ways, you now interact with like never before. Others in your former peer group with whom you interacted in a more relaxed and open exchange are now more distant and guarded as the impact of your new position takes hold. Those who deny or fail to fully understand this may find themselves surprised with regard to their expectations of friendship during a crucial test. It is especially acute where management comes from the same general labor pool and may be closely associated off the job. *A former mentor often espoused an old truism that said, "the quickest way to lose a friend is either go to work for them or borrow money from them."* It is probably true more often than not.

The very nature of a new manager's position will require a degree of mutually accepted workday distance between you and the now subordinate friend to avoid any taint of impropriety or preferential treatment. It can be a difficult balancing act—especially when it comes to directing and evaluating the friend's performance. One thing is certain, it's going to change the nature of your friendship to some degree—like it or not.

One must deal with this reality by talking it over with the friend. Do not assume a colleague understands what is expected. The virtue of a true friendship should be the standard to address this challenge. If your friend was promoted over you, wouldn't you want the friend to succeed? Shouldn't your friend wish the same for you and act accordingly? Especially since both you and your long standing, yet now subordinate, friend will be the focus of inordinate scrutiny by others. Any preferential treatment of a friend in an official capacity will only undermine your validity and effectiveness with others. It should not be what a virtuous friend would want to have happen.

Other Considerations

What is your relationship with your position? How committed are you to the ideals and expectations of your newly acquired rank and its authority? (*Refer to the oath taking in Loyalty section.*) Understanding 'role' is important to this concern. How do the friend's expectations pair with your expectations for and the obligation to your new job responsibilities? A crucible will only intensify the quandary stemming from your sense of allegiance to a friend and the commitment to your new position's role.

In truth, few friends live up to the ideal under all circumstances. Some relationships are unequal. How <u>you</u> interpret friendship may not be viewed quite the same as your friend. While you view your friendship from a more virtuous perspective, the friend may be looking at it from a useful or for pleasure view.

When dealing with a crucible involving a close friend's predicament, your analysis should boil down to the friend's intent behind the circumstances. This is important for extending any benefit of doubt. Were his or her intentions reasonable, well intended, even excusable, or do they stem from a reckless, wanton, or a conscious wrong? In other words the friend's conscious wrong doing (*driving while drunk, padding expenses, contriving evidence, etc.*) is definitely outside the realm of a true friendship. It's not that they did something stupid, but were recklessly or intentionally wrong. Rather than accept the responsibility and consequence of their own actions, they may try to put the onus on you to abet their behavior. It is abuse and misuse of this special relationship. <u>A true friend takes responsibility for his or her actions and faces the consequences to avoid entangling the other friend.</u> The other true friend can likewise openly and substantively support the friend without abetting or making matters worse.

Honesty should be your only course in this kind of dilemma. The best solution to whatever you face is to go with the truth (facts) as you know it. Any benefit of doubt should be based on facts that support your assumption, and not what you wish them to be. Try to view every issue with a long term perspective—when the intensity and passion of the moment have faded. In other words, instead of choosing to abet behavior through devious means, consider what may be a more preferable longer term benefit. (*If only we'd been truthful earlier, we'd only be facing administrative action instead of being prosecuted criminally.*) Sometimes making the painful decision you know is right— what you feel in your gut—at the risk of losing the intensity of the friendship in the shorter term is the real basis of a more virtuous friendship. The best friend is the one who confronts the weakness or incompetence of the other friend <u>before</u> a potential crucible, and helps him or her overcome the deficiency.

A final consideration should be understood. Sometimes friendships fail. It happens. Maybe your friend's expectations are unreasonable and greater than what you can deliver. It may be hard to accept, but when it comes to your personal sense of self-worth, integrity, and what you know—deep down—to be right, then this kind of entwining friend may not be worth the price.

The Quandary

The late film actress, Elizabeth Taylor, once said, "You find out who your real friends are when you're involved in a scandal." She was lamenting those who shied away from supporting her in time of need. It is reminiscent of an oft used quote, "Hey, what are friends for …?" It implies that friends are supposed to defend and bolster one another's position or situation—<u>regardless</u> of the circumstances.

It also carries an unfair implication of betrayal, especially for those who know or suspect something they should not or cannot accept or defend, yet are compelled to do so. Betrayal is a powerfully coercive word. No one wants to be tagged with that kind of reputation. However, like all bottom line issues, it will take courage to do what's right—especially when others have already crossed the line into deception and obstruction in a misguided attempt to *help* the friend or cohort.

One may feel compelled to protect something they sense is more important than the perceived outcome of the issue at hand. For example, the survival of a colleague's career or the organization's image may seem more urgent than the challenge posed by a less knowledge-able or disrespected source *(an outside agency or superior with little experi-ence, or distrusted internal affairs person, etc.).*

Friendship—even just familiarity—can combine with loyalty to be-come the building blocks for an almost innate, unwritten code of si-lence or deception. This happens when people in an intensely cohe-sive environment feel obligated to remain loyal to each other due to unique circumstances—whether you are a friend of the accused or not. It could stem from a belief that what you do is so unique that no other person except a colleague could truly understand your situation.

It's one thing to believe in another's integrity based on what you ac-tually know. However, it is quite another to suspect or know of al-leged indiscretions and conspire to abet them in the name of a mis-used label of friendship. It is especially egregious when a consistently marginal or problem employee reaps the <u>undeserved</u> benefit from an alliance with others because of a misunderstood or overvalued notion of loyalty and friendship.

Let's go back to the incident at the beginning of this chapter where a friend punched a secured offender. You may have initially viewed it as an emotional reaction and not a deliberately brutal act. The test began with what you—the supervisor—did with that observation. What the friend did—denigrating and punching a secured offender—may be rationalized from an emotional perspective when weighed against the difficulty encountered in gaining control. *(An emotional reaction is usually spontaneous, immediate, autonomic, etc., versus deliberate, which is unprovoked, intentional, wanton, with malice, etc.)* Maybe your friend sustained some blows from the offender. This is where past experience, entrenched bias, and questionable circumstances can rat-tle around the decision making rationale of many trying to balance what is officially required with what may be a cynical sense of reality.

The offender was a career criminal versus the qualities of a career officer in the heat of an emotionally charged situation, something you feel others (inquisitors) may not appreciate or understand. You imagine the potential fallout— overreaction to a mistake versus what could become politically charged with consequences far beyond a reasonable and appropriate resolution.

You may sense a need to protect your friend against something you feel does not deserve a more official level of action, and that your counsel and his apology at the scene was sufficient. However, was it really enough? What kind of help will your friend expect <u>now</u> that it has become an official inquiry? Will it be to further ignore, minimize, or purposely withhold the truthful events of that situation? It becomes a <u>bottom line</u> battle between reason and emotion. It will involve a clash between your commitment to your role, the law, responsibility, and what you feel may be an unfair or inappropriate outcome for a friend.

You may question the seriousness of the incident in relation to what would be a proper supervisory action to correct or discipline? *It may seem easier to overlook the issue and hope no one ever questions the act. However, in today's video-omnipotent world, you may be risking more severe consequences for others in need of your loyalty because of a friend's indiscretion.*

So the question becomes should you have taken more official action against your friend? Did the verbal reprimand and later not telling the superior *really* serve your friend's best interest? *And* what about the equally valued interests of others involved in the fracas? In other words, a less official action at the outset (undocumented verbal admonishment) may have put other officers at risk because of a later temptation or coercion to deny seeing what they had observed.

Time for Questions!

It is crucible time—you are being asked to provide information that could be damaging to a friend, and you know others have covered up. How much support can one reasonably extend to a friend that may undermine or put others at undue risk? What is best for the friend versus convenient or enabling? If you were to lie for a friend and it is discovered—exposing you to severe consequences—how would this factor into your commitments to others not involved? If you're going to stick your neck out for a friend involved in a reckless or conscious wrong, does it *really* fit the true meaning of friendship? What is the basis of the friendship you seek to defend? Is it for pleasure, usefulness, or for virtue? Can you be truthful—even though it is damaging—and still be friends? Why not take responsibility for your decision to just admonish, and then explain (justify) your actions versus omitting or lying out of fear of being second guessed or risking the friendship?

The alternative is doing something more official at the outset (letter to file, maybe a temporary reassignment or an anger control course, etc.) and being more truthful to the boss. It could very well lessen the likelihood of a later crucible. Other witnessing officers—knowing it was handled officially—could avoid being drawn into a blue wall or similar kind of deceptive scenario.

Is the risk you feel compelled to take for the friend justified? Maybe the consequences aren't as dire as you imagine. Are the circumstances of the challenge truly worthy of the risk? What are you prepared to risk for the sake of friendship, and will it ever be enough? *The officer who punched the secured offender fell victim to what a professional should not. He or she exceeded their authority in your presence without regard to how it impacts you and others.*

Is it a true friend who expects a risky favor for the sake of their self preservation at the expense of yours? Or, could it be one who avoids involving you above his or her well being? On the other hand, what kind of friend abets and compounds the issue by adding another wrong to the original one, thereby enabling, or possibly deepening the friend's woes?

When one friend shares a secret or indiscretion with another, and that friend is then faced with having to answer an official inquiry regarding that knowledge, will the wrong friend expect the other to lie or mislead the lawful source of that challenge? Can the queried friend be honest to inquirers and still be a friend? A lot will depend on how each one views or understands what true friendship should be.

This is not to say one should run to the boss to report every indiscretion or problem you handled a tad less than what may be officially required. But it's good to consider these questions when grappling with a serious predicament; one that may require a more official, responsible supervisory action initially to keep it from becoming a crucible later—even for a friend..

The crucible!

The ultimate test for a manager comes when he or she has to answer to a lawful authority on what you or another did or didn't do in regard to an issue. Are you prepared to take responsibility for your actions and expect the same from others—even if it's detrimental to both yourself and the welfare of a friend? Remember, consequences tend to rise in severity with each additional step needed to resolve something that has been thwarted by choosing any value over honesty.

What you observe, hear, or feel, and then <u>what you decide to do</u> is a critical juncture. <u>That next step determines your culpability</u>. Will it entail ignoring or abetting? Or taking the much harder, but more responsible action? Most crucibles do not evolve from innocent or well-intended mistakes. They grow out of improperly mitigated reckless, irresponsible, or consciously committed wrongs. The quality and value of 'courage' will elbow its way into this decision process.

WHAT *CAN* YOU DO AS A FRIEND?

What can one friend offer the other during a crucible and stay honest at the same time? You can honestly offer condolences, forgiveness, and moral support throughout their hardship. You may also help by affording or arranging something that can <u>legitimately</u> ease or correct the problem (appropriate advice, counsel, referrals, etc.).

In the example at the beginning of this chapter, when your friend punched a secured offender, you could have engaged the harder path—the one that may have entailed something more official than telling him to "cool off" (especially if he is suspected or known to have done something similar before), and been more forthcoming to the Chief when he or she asked.

These are tough issues to deal with. They are the kind of decisions and actions that come with the territory of managing—especially during times of controversy and conflict. They require good communication. In other words, while taking a more official action, you can reassure the friend of your continued friendship—that while you will stand by him or her, you must *also* fulfill the responsibilities you have sworn to do. Most *true* friends will not only understand, but respect you for it, too. For when it comes to aiding through deception—<u>that</u>

should be the bottom line not crossed. The rationale is "I will stand by you, but not join you." One should never feel guilty for not doing enough if what was expected surpassed your bottom line.

Bottom line—you should still be friends without having to commit a wrong for the other. And, if that is not good enough for the friend, so be it. It is the bottom line you're not going to cross. Period!! In a culture where powerful forces of coercion come to bear (to be considered disloyal and ostracized or isolated by many others is a harsh consequence)—then it certainly becomes a matter of courage to stand up for what you know is right in spite of the consequences.

However, bottom line and courage are often one and the same.

PART III

Keeping the Workplace Professional

CHAPTER 11

Keeping the Workplace Professional

A professional work environment (PWE) has nothing to do with how new or modern one's office space or patrol vehicle is, or how unique the logo or general reputation may *seem* to be. A PWE can exist anywhere, on the dock at a waste transfer station or the precinct house on the meanest street in America, and yet be noticeably absent in a plush, airy corporate office atop the largest building in the city. That's because it begins and ends with management. Managers set the tone and tenor for all workplace activity.

In professional work environments everyone's focus of attention and effort is to fulfill mission and goals in a climate of civility, equality, dignity, and a sense of fulfillment for employees. It is free of hostility, pettiness, mistrust, fear, secrecy, greed, favoritism, negativity, exploitation and many other workplace negatives.

Professional managers foster and nurture this kind of right-minded environment. They exude competence, rationale, and decorum, all of which discourage daily discourse and misunderstanding. They smile, encourage, support, recognize, and deal *respectfully* with everyone— from the janitor to the CEO. They don't foster or laugh at

denigrating or off-color jokes, or use nicknames or anything other
than the person's proper title. They correct constructively in private
and maintain open avenues of communication and adequate processes for conflict resolution. Their subordinates enjoy respect, recognition, and appreciation. Professional managers lead by example.
They believe in and are fully committed to their role. It's not an image. **It is a base from which an image evolves.**

It may have been fun during your days as a first line employee to join
in the general banter and exchange of fellow employees—engaging
light hearted "digs" at someone's mistakes or eccentricities. It was
part of the group equilibrium—infusing serious labor with a modest
balance of humor and lighthearted interplay, which helps maintain
variety and interest in a daily focus on what some may consider me-
nial, repetitious, or routine. However, as a manager it is important to
carefully constrain such activity in order to ensure inclusiveness (sensitivity to *everyone's* situation) in your new position. How you used to
tease a friend or peer in your previous position is no longer acceptable because of your responsibility regarding how others may perceive your actions. This doesn't mean you must become aloof and
indifferent, or become the model of a saint, but just ensure any good
natured banter or exchange is not at the expense of another, or used
to undermine the organization's hierarchy or purpose.

We *all* have biases that impact the way we view the world. We are
going to like some people more than others. *You* may have an aversion to someone of a particular ilk being a member of your organization. However, an important part of a PWE is the ability of the manager to be aware of and stifle whatever character faults or prejudicial
inklings he or she may have for the sake of the mission. Radio personalities, salesmen, and others who rely on interpersonal skills to
survive in business learn to suppress personal issues in order to
maintain the persona needed for effective interaction. *An unstable*

marriage, mounting bills, teenage children, etc., can pre-occupy one's attention span and mood on occasion. Avoid these pitfalls by consciously trying to leave your personal faults and troubles at the door.

This should apply to a manager in *any* kind of environment, even those where upper level management tolerates—or street level challenges give rise to—a climate of defensiveness or disquietude *the overbearing, hard charging supervisor building a tough guy reputation based on cutting corners, unreasonable aggression, exceeding authority, and bullying others to follow suit.* When one understands and accepts the basic tenets of a PWE, it's just a matter of adjusting one's own professional bearing accordingly. In other words, a PWE persona can be applied to <u>any</u> position, regardless of the larger work environment (like an oasis of reason in a desert of chaos). Granted, it's much easier when upper management backs you up. However, the legitimacy of one's position (rank), coupled with the power of his or her persuasive convictions (character), can overcome—or at least moderate—the *noise* of an otherwise unprofessional environment. Having a good grasp of role and a real time awareness of a solid bottom line helps provide the new manager with a proper direction to pursue.

The Alternative

<u>Un</u>professional work environments lack direction and cohesiveness. They are filled with bias, adversity, low morale, and other characteristics, which make employees uncomfortable. There is little or no recourse for remedy inside the organization. You'll find people working against each other and limiting individual potential. It's a place where bullying, caustic, and uncaring comments (Suck it up, fella!), and other shenanigans are tolerated and sometimes even encouraged.

This is especially true in organizations that overindulge the tough guy bravado of a male dominant culture. It encourages a level of physicality, insensitivity, and confrontation to propagate a misguided self image of *machismo*. Granted, law enforcers deal with bad people in tough areas, but the interpretation of "tough" can be somewhat subjective. Toughness should never be styled only on the physical, vocal, or dominating demeanor of one or a few, but on the power of the law and the whole of the organization enforcing it. Besides, the toughest are those who stand fast to righteous principle in the face of overwhelming pressure to do otherwise. They do what is right, regardless of how threatening or harsh the consequences.

In law enforcement where certain environments (volatile and hostile neighborhoods) or assignments (undercover, riot control, special operations) can be overly adversarial, confrontational, or even violent, regular attention must be paid to help moderate or dissipate the inevitable tension, cynicism, and defensiveness.

One of the most challenging features in law enforcement is the encroachment of cynicism and defensiveness into the law enforcer's persona. Cynics have a tendency to lump all clientele (public served) into one adversarial category. Unfortunately it is too often a two-way street. No one sees a police car drive up and thinks "Isn't that nice, a policeman's coming to visit." When any law enforcement official and ordinary citizen meet, there is a natural tendency for both to be cautious of the other's intentions. It is a natural barrier to open communication that one or the other, or both, must make an extra effort to overcome.

Any lack of organizational effort to address this subtle, but powerful, dilemma puts greater responsibility on the first line manager to pick up the slack. They must try to empathize, counsel, coach, and direct employees *frequently* enough to help ameliorate the cynical view one may be acquiring about the public they serve. While some employees may feel it is none of the manager's business, it won't hurt to encourage them to expand their social network. This gets done by engaging in activities and interacting with law abiding citizenry on a regular basis to help counter balance this kind of negative drift. It is an important byproduct of a vigorous community policing effort, and helps lessen overexposure to community negatives.

CHAPTER 12

Overreaction

Another toxic feature of law enforcement is the adrenalin pumping situation that can challenge <u>anyone's</u> commitment to professionalism. High speed chases, grappling for a gun, shots fired, vicious taunts and affronts, etc. can unearth emotional reactions never imagined until it actually happens. Preparing for it is one thing; actually experiencing it is another.

Unnecessary use of anything, whether it's force, intimidation, degradation, or whatever, seldom achieves its intended effect. A noteworthy old adage says *"A strength overused ultimately becomes a weakness."* There are physical, verbal, visual, and visceral experiences that can challenge even the most professional persona. Professionalism is much easier to define and employ in a controlled and rational environment, but can become fragile very quickly in the chaotic and dangerous realm of enforcing the law. There are situations that can quickly unearth deep-seated and suppressed urges for retribution, vengeance, and recompense, which lie in everyone's character, no matter how good they try to be.

Those who, either emotionally or deliberately, employ tactics to satisfy any kind of emotional urge for retribution or recompense seldom accomplish their aim anyway. *Yes, the offender may wish he hadn't punched you in the face after he was pummeled repeatedly by you and others, but—deep down—will likely feel the pathos that he or she was justified in their offending action.* In some radical factions it's a badge of honor to incite overreaction to undermine an opponent's claim to legitimacy or higher ground. It is certainly the tactical strategy of some activists touting a purposely disruptive agenda.

<u>The control of emotion, the tempering of passion's overzealousness, and containing the vindictiveness of frustration are marks of a true professional.</u>

However, no other career—outside of military combat—challenges this capability more than law enforcement.

Guidelines Galore

Every officer is trained with regard to the laws and ethics surrounding the use of force. There are video programs recreating tense 'Shoot Don't Shoot' scenarios and role playing, which try to simulate actual examples of exasperating and/or deadly confrontations. Batons, sprays, Tasers, and other implements help balance whatever disparities exist between an offender's physique, armament, and ability to endanger, and an officer's capability to detain, control, and take the offender into custody. They are important tools for use of force necessary to accomplish duties.

All of these processes help to enhance proper procedure and behavior while reason and control are still in place. That is until the offender suddenly grabs the handle of your gun. Then everything can unravel. While guidelines and training educate and regulate officers in the proper use of force, even the best training will never fully prepare one for the sensation of the *actual* event. That's because what's missing in any kind of written guideline or contrived scenario is the shocking sense of imminent death or grave physical harm, which an *actual* event can trigger. The primordial urge for survival can suddenly erupt and dominate one's consciousness. It stimulates a rush of adrenaline and autonomic reflexes, which often continue into the immediate aftermath of the event itself.

The sensation is akin to drowning. The instinct to survive can have the drowning person frantically clawing at *anything* for breath—even their rescuer. However, when fighting for your life with an offender, it is in the immediate aftermath, when you regain control and begin to realize you will survive *(and adrenalin is still coursing your veins),* that emotions of retribution, anger, even hate can find their way into your reflexes. This is true even in those situations where the offender has taken you to your emotional limit, and then just gives up, thereby depriving the officer of any kind of compensatory action he or she may emotionally feel would somehow balance out the equation. *A secured offender kicks an officer in the groin and head-butts another. It can be argued this kind of situation is an occupational hazard—that a professional should be prepared for and accept it as part of the job. However, even the most professional officer on the receiving end of the assault will experience negative emotions that will be difficult to contain.*

A car chase is another example. When the reckless, wanton, and sometimes bullet punctuated actions imperil the safety and welfare of pursuing officers and innocent bystanders, it can push adrenalin induced physiological responses to their limit. Passion for immediate retribution *(a desire for the offender to "feel" the fear and pain he caused you)* can churn in one's gut. Waiting for justice isn't quite there yet in this highly charged emotional state. This should be the target area for managers to frequently address in training and during coaching or counseling.

So, while a shout, slap or kick may be understood from an emotional standpoint, it must be frequently emphasized that this kind of reaction to an offender's ploy is not what a professional should fall victim. (*It means the offender has drawn the retaliating officers into his or her realm*). Such actions in our video-omnipotent world only put at risk the appropriate and longer term extent of justice to be meted out later. It requires a conscious effort to be aware of and to control your emotional triggers, exercise restraint, and think clearly in the face of adversity. (*A secured offender stands rigid at the open door of your vehicle, refusing to be placed inside. Thinking of a less impetuous way—one officer pulling on his belt from behind, while the other pushes his stomach and pulls down his head—may be better than spraying, tasing, or punching to overcome a nominal form of resistance.*)

Verbal Assault!

Sometimes words can hurt, too! (*During an interview with detectives, a suspect in the murder of a police officer expresses glee over the officer's demise.*) While the threat of imminent danger is not present, the elements of extreme spite, defiance, even hate can stir emotion into an urge for verbal or physical release. There are people who are very good at saying things that can quickly stab at the core of one's emotion. (*Watch how much harder the judge bangs the gavel when disrespected by a defendant.*) Open defiance like 'getting up in your face,' jabbing a finger into the chest, or other aggressive, denigrating gestures and sinister threats (*I know where you live ...*) can raise one's blood pressure and fluster one's self control almost as readily as those from a physical assault. *A former mentor once advised me there exist street wise "smart-asses" out there who could provoke any professional trained in conflict resolution into a fit of rage within minutes of meeting them.(I have found that to be true on more than one occasion.)*

Law enforcers are normally rule-oriented people. They believe in what they do and are trained to maintain order and control in difficult situations. But, when the offender purposely urinates in the patrol car, spits at you, or looks you directly in the eye while menacingly saying "F*you Officer so and so," it is going to provoke lamentable emotional urges that are difficult to suppress. These are real life examples of exasperating situations that strike at the heart of professionalism in a volatile and chaotic work environment. However, as often taught in the martial arts, it's not so much the techniques of blocks, kicks, and punches that wins the fight. It is more the ability to control and use them effectively during close and intense physical exchanges. This kind of strategic control is what most often comes out on top.

Time to become 'Clinical'

To be clinical is to have the ability to disengage, depersonalize, and divorce emotion from your assessment of and addressing the issue at hand. While it is easier said than done, it *can* and must be done. Doctors, judges, auditors, interrogators, Special Ops personnel, and others employ it to ensure the purity, legitimacy, and effectiveness in certain aspects of their job. It means paring away all the extraneous noise that can impact the best way to handle an emotionally challenging event. Noise includes the urges for blame, retribution, recompense, vengefulness, or any other emotional influence that can detract from one's focus for accomplishing a required outcome. One point to remember is the offender is more often not disrespecting *you*—he or she probably doesn't know you as an individual—but the authority your uniform represents, which you care about as well. *In other words, don't take the conflict personally.*

One must consciously place professional standards against emotional urges. The despicable act is not yours to personalize, but to address in a clinical manner. Training, experience, and job skills should dominate one's conscious effort to resolve any distressful situation at hand. *A pilot trying to regain control of a disabled aircraft will focus strictly on what he or she is trained to do and not what passengers are screaming, who's responsible for the malfunction, or blaming the airplane, etc. Likewise, once the pilot regains control, it would only entail further risk to pound the instrument panel out of frustration or anger.*

Police officers often consciously ignore or minimize the stench of a decomposing body or the gore of a terrible accident. They do this by concentrating on what must be done procedurally to investigate the crime or resolve the issue. The same kind of conditioning must be employed when facing a consternating, obstinate, or despicable personality.

The harsher, more confrontational the episode, the more clinical one must become to control the emotion of the moment. A shove or punch, a video camera in the face, a horrifically abused child, no remorse from one responsible for a monstrous act, and the list goes on and on of actions employed by offenders that can trigger these deep emotions.

Some hold the cynical view that courts don't weigh sufficiently an offender's wanton disrespect or resistance towards the arresting officer, which feeds a feeling of nonchalance which allow occasional acts of "roadside justice" to occur.

To keep negatives at bay, one must be aware of and consciously work to keep (preempt) them from interfering with the issue to be resolved. *Rioters violently protesting police brutality—one wearing a T-shirt emblazoned with "Cops Suck," while spewing hate directed at responding officers. This noise can surround the professional issue (restoring order) and impede its being addressed appropriately*. Planning, tactics, and execution should be conducted with the singular goal of restoring order. Officers should be coached to consciously suppress emotional urges, which lead to retribution or a desire for immediate punishment, and tune out the noise.

Any subject or offender, regardless of what he or she has done, said, or threatened to do, is an entity to be dealt with according to the training you've had, tools that you have, and common sense. The offending person pushing your buttons should become a professional challenge. It should include efforts to defuse or lessen the volatility of the matter versus meeting disagreement and confrontation with equal or greater measures. In other words, one must consciously lump their (offender's) despicability into a lesser category to be ignored for the sake of a professional outcome. Any protagonist's verbal attempt to unearth your emotions should be considered noise that must be filtered out from what is necessary to resolve the issue. Once an offender is under control and secured, there is no justification that will ever pass muster with a jury for any kind of overreaction or recompense—period!

It must be frequently coached that a big part of professionalism is the exercise of restraint & control of emotion in the face of adversity. This is especially important for officers predisposed to overreaction. *Very often this kind of employee is well known by others (peers) through past experience, bragging, war stories, about how he or she treats people.* Officers prone to this behavior, or rookies who overreact to gain approval from peers should be addressed immediately, then periodically with face-to-face coaching sessions. It's not enough to be taught in the academy when first hired, and then just let it ride 'til the actual event occurs.

The harsher the conditions on the street, the more pro-active management must be to provide employees a means to vent and destress. These realities—left to their own resolution—can lead to defensiveness, disgruntlement, even paranoia, which can show up later as problem employee issues and incidents of domestic discourse and violence. It's not enough to advise everyone to "be careful out there," or ask, "Are you okay?" and leave it at that. Any kind of unsettling experience should have regular follow up with personal attention. It is important for managers to differentiate what is understandably emotional versus uncharacteristically deliberate, and how overreaction—under any circumstance—can impact <u>all</u> of law enforcement under certain conditions.

Post incident debriefs and counseling should be commonplace. While it can be time consuming and expensive to engage this kind of approach, so are the costs of the consequences. *One cannot overemphasize the need for officers to frequently decompress, to have a means by which frustration, anxiety, and fear can be brought to the surface and allowed to dissipate in some measure. It can be a gym facility, a punching bag, extracurricular activities, impromptu bull sessions for some levity, or organized uninhibited group sessions to discuss the challenges of the day, which can help ease pent up emotion. Stifled emotion is the precursor to just about every serious employee problem issue you'll face. What can be done about it? Or, better yet, what is being done about it?*

Other Concerns

Most workplace violence situations have a history of evolving and escalating conflict paved with subtle indicators that are either ignored or rationalized away by the inadvertent observer. A sudden display of anger by an employee may be forgotten too soon after an apology without thinking through the possible reasons for such a display. It's not so much a matter of immediate intervention as it is a <u>strategic consciousness</u> that is required. In other words, it may not be enough to pull two people apart to cool off. It may require a more in-depth analysis to resolve what may be a deeper issue smoldering beneath a seemingly normal surface.

Incorporating diversity and change into the daily equilibrium and productivity of the organization creates huge challenges for management. One of the most important parts of a manager's role is to facilitate change in the workplace and overcome the inevitable resistance to anything new. Managers themselves may not like the way things may be going either. However, if the change is imbedded in law and propriety, it is an essential part of your role to subjugate personal feelings for the success of the mission you've sworn yourself to uphold.

Television and movies too often portray law enforcers as troubled, cynical, combative, and abusive. The great majority are the low key, consistent, methodical, persevering men and women who are rule-oriented, with a keen sense of responsibility and professionalism. They maintain good relationships with others, vary their occupation with outside interests, and deliver professional results. They remain calm in the face of adversity, and don't let the weakness or negativism of others drag them into the same arena.

CHAPTER 13

Profanity and Posturing?

Watch your thoughts for they become words. Watch your words for they become actions. Watch your actions for they become habits. Watch your habits for they become character. Watch your character for it becomes destiny ...

Frank Outlaw, Supermarket Magnate

The use of profanity in our culture is an everyday reality. Some terms are almost colloquial in their use, i.e., damn, screw it, pissed, hell, sucks, son-of-a-b***h, etc. It is rare to encounter anyone who hasn't used or uttered an expletive or two under stressful conditions. However, too much fuels an UN-professional environment. It can accentuate and make worse the normal, relatively minor everyday discourse that occurs between employees and clientele. It is seldom heard in the professional work environment, and if it is—it's never used to denigrate or humiliate another. *Besides, excess profanity is like a tantrum— the flushed faced, fist pounding, spittle laced shouting at others. While it may induce immediate results and actions from some, it mostly shows lack of control to others that—over time—undermines the persona of the manager and the respect he or she needs to be more effective.* It is important to remember that management sets the tone and tenor of subordinate actions, and if you are prone to denigrating profanity it is likely your subordinates will treat others in kind—especially the recipient (general public) of their purpose.

However, whatever the intent of the profanity, negative colloquialism, or derogatory term, it is when it is preceded by a personal or possessive pronoun (you or your) that a very strong undertone of disrespect gets communicated. *"I want everyone's butt here by six o'clock,"* versus, *"I want all you humps here by ..."* It is one thing when used to accentuate a point as a general exclamation, but quite another when it becomes personalized and used to denigrate or humiliate another.

The more graphic and anatomical, the more coarse and disrespectful it becomes to all within earshot. This is especially true when dealing with any kind of consternating personality or situation. A purposely antagonistic employee, prisoner, suspect, complainant, are examples of those who can push emotional buttons to their limit. In a video omnipotent world, profanity can be a self defeating habit, which can risk a preferred outcome with unnecessary and sometimes provocative noise.

Always keep in the mind the longer term—sometimes more abstract—effects of your actions. Like in the old movies, the fabled "fatherly" looking cop on the beat, the one who knows the neighborhood and encourages more than commands. *"Now move along, fellas (loiterers), you shouldn't be out here this time of night."* While it certainly sounds hokey and unrealistic in today's world, it is equally unfitting to shout *"Move a_ _hole, or I'll ..."* The first may elicit laughter and even derision, but the latter will certainly stir emotions of defiance, dislike—even hate. Which (rationally) serves a longer term better interest of the department's purpose (mission)?

Also, there is a high degree of expectation of professional conduct from those being served, underline regardless of their social, economic, or cultural climate. Working tough neighborhoods can evoke a feeling one must adjust to, for example, what may be an overly profane local lingo, or how locals react behaviorally to you or interrelate with one another. Some people may *seem* to react favorably to your effort to fit in with high fives and knuckle bumps, but deep down most will see it for what it really is—pandering with ulterior motives. The unfortunate side effect for falling victim to this inclination is that overuse of profanity can back draft into your office and home life, too.

The bottom line should be to make a conscious effort to drop profanity from your workplace persona, or at least try to limit its use, and to ensure it is never directed at or personalized to another. Overuse will detract from the general perception of you as a professional.

Profanity is absolutely <u>unacceptable</u> in any officially written or recorded communication, whether a letter, report, radio transmission, email, text, twitter, etc., unless used to describe or record pertinent dialogue for evidentiary purposes. Any kind of extraneous profanity that gets <u>recorded</u> invariably undermines the desired outcome of one's efforts, especially when the communication gets exposed in court or becomes public. *Envision sitting in a jury box when deciding a course of action. Ask yourself, how will my emotional outburst or illicit action look to a lay person deciding the case? Because, if it doesn't pass muster there, then all is for naught.*

Managers must constantly communicate their commitment to high standards. It is an essential part of the role they sought, attained, and must now <u>fulfill</u>.

Posturing

It is one thing when working undercover, but quite another when conducting the business of professionalism in the normal workplace environment. Don't try to be what you're not. Trying to emulate, mimic, or assume a different persona based on an obsequious urge to fit in with the mannerisms or lingo of the group you manage will never enhance your ability to get the job done <u>through others</u>. *It is seen often in gender overreach—females, and in some cases milder, less aggressive males displaying bravado or tough guy mannerisms when their true nature is the opposite. It is often seen in a rookie's over aggressiveness for what he or she feels will impress their more seasoned peers.* It will invariably be seen for what it is—an unnatural attempt to gain attention, pandering, a weakness, or even an affront to those who observe it. It is certainly not expected or welcome from those being managed.

Your role is to acclimate to and adopt the principles and values of the position you occupy in their purest sense—even if you've risen from the group you now must manage. *Acclimating to role is acquiring characteristics important to personal and professional growth and leadership qualities. Posturing is assuming superficial or unnatural behaviors you think must be done to belong, which will make you popular or acceptable, but takes away from your ability to manage effectively.* It's like growing up in New England and trying to mimic the regional speech characteristics of the Deep South or Midwest—or vice versa. Who couldn't see through that?

It will never be the superficiality of assuming a different persona to fit in, but your commitment and courage to fulfill your role with respect and civility, which will ultimately gain the respect you need as an effective leader. *To stand up and call for 'time out' at the stag party that is getting out of hand or the overreaction to an offender's defiance. To stop the activity that is descending into inappropriate behavior. It may mean you have to become the drag on the party, being booed and heckled for the greater good and what is right.* Don't let anything dissuade you from doing what's needed and right. So, stay true to the role you must fulfill (be consistent) and manage and lead accordingly rather than going along or fitting in. Doing what is right may not win you popularity, but being popular doesn't mean you're managing right (correctly). Real managers do what is right and not what makes them popular.

CHAPTER 14

Alcohol and Drugs

The incident elevating this problem to upper management's or the media's attention is too late. There should have been earlier intervention. In most incidents involving serious substance abuse, there were telltale signs leading up to the car accident or embarrassing public display, which were ignored, abetted or the butt of jokes and innuendo along the way. The reluctance to initiate any official action for something that may be embarrassing to the individual, or negatively impact the employee's future credibility (disclosure matter), should <u>not</u> be an issue at the necessary time. Do what should be done—get the person help. Deal with the fallout later.

The availability and sophistication of human resource options have expanded over the years to a point where most law enforcement agencies either have or can access professional counseling and human relation resources. The concern should be with the period of time preceding whatever event or incident generated the official intervention or referral. It pertains to those times where employees overindulging certain substances were first noticed or suspected of doing so. It's a time when the true value of loyalty and friendship *should* play a role. It is during the time friends or cohorts ignored, placated, enabled, or actually covered up an individual's descent into alcohol or substance abuse. There are too many examples where colleagues and management knew of a pending problem with an employee abusing substances—especially alcohol, and did nothing.

As discussed in the previous chapters, the *true* meaning of loyalty and friendship would have colleagues and managers confronting the abuser sooner rather than later—to help he or she avoid further descent into self-destructive behavior. It should be done with the abuser's <u>true</u> best interest at heart—even when told to "mind your own business." The *real* friend confronts and tries to redirect the friend to abstain even at the risk of lowering the level of intimacy in the relationship. (*Has anyone thought about organizing an intervention with other concerned colleagues—to sit down with the abuser to express their concern and offer to help them change? You don't have to be a trained psychologist to do that—just a real friend.*)

People who overindulge in *anything* need help that resolves their affliction <u>before</u> it becomes an addiction—not the laughter or war stories and bravado that abets or enables their behavior. The true friend and real loyalist is the one with courage and foresight to confront the reality of the situation *<u>before</u>* it becomes an incident that places the abuser and many others in a difficult situation.

CHAPTER 15

Sex in the Workplace

It's going to happen, even in work environments where clearly ar-
ticulated personal relationship policies and guidelines exist. Its power
dwells right at the core of our being. It can manifest itself in all kinds
of bizarre and nebulous behavior, from ogling, vane primping, un-
couth mannerisms, and inappropriate dress, to the sometimes
outrageous acts of excessive vulgarity, voyeurism, indelicate touching
or groping, and beyond.

History is replete with idols, heroes, clergy, CEOs, and world leaders
who tarnished lifetimes of achievement while under the siren song of
sexual allure. In law enforcement there are many examples of good
officers enticed into illicit relationships with colleagues, victims, suspects, and informants. So, while trying to prevent inappropriate sexually compelled behavior during work hours with policy guidelines and
other forms of indoctrination is a good thing, <u>it's still going to hap-
pen</u> on occasion.

While there is nothing management can do about the reasons (why)
an injudicious attraction or deviance occurs, it *can* do something
about the *where* and *when*. It should not occur in the workplace, and
the involved employee(s) must understand the reasoning behind this

position. So, let's explore some options for dealing with sex *when* it breaks out in the work place.

Real Romance

Romance (love) in the workplace can be an amusing diversion (many find a spouse in the workplace), a temporary nuisance, or, in some cases, a very serious problem. This is especially true in law enforcement where weapons are part of the daily mix. It's one thing when two unencumbered consenting adults are attracted to one another and are discreet and professional. However, it is quite another when one or both are already elsewhere committed, responsible for assessing either's performance, and/or compelled by any kind of deviant or prurient urge. It can induce jealousy, hurt feelings, debasing embarrassment, and behaviors that manifest themselves as serious job inhibitors and even workplace violence. It is an area that many too often tiptoe around, except to engage humor, rumor, or innuendo.

It is important for management to understand the nature and inevitability of this phenomenon, and not only handle it with genuine sensitivity, civility, and privacy, but to avoid the pitfall themselves. This is especially true when supervisor and subordinate end up in each other's arms.

When a manager feels the urge to push a professional relationship to something more personal or intimate, it's time for him or her to STOP AND THINK! When tempted to engage or be drawn into an illicit intimate relationship with a subordinate one should do some self reflection regarding their commitment to role, and then adjust the situation accordingly. *The manager who pays too much attention or is seen overvisiting with a subordinate will create unease throughout the unit. Subordinates are very perceptive about imbalances in a manager's routine.* It is time to remember the *craps table analogy*—the untenable gamble of putting your reputation, family stability, and all of your efforts to get where you are professionally on just <u>one</u> number (*the immediate infatuation*), and rolling the dice. That is not a gamble; it's just plain stupid.

Regardless of how professional one thinks he or she is, when a manager is involved with another under his or her purview, it will invariably fuel suspicion and distrust among other employees and quickly undermine the credibility of his or her role as a supervisor. It is a situation that *has* to change. Even if it is a legitimate romance, adjustments are still necessary. A true professional will accept whatever measures are necessary to rectify it. *Like Britain's King Edward VIII, who abdicated his right to the throne to marry an American commoner, Wallis Simpson, in 1937, sometimes it comes down to a choice between one or the other.* One of the pair will have to be reassigned accordingly. If it is a legitimate romance, it should not have a punitive tone or tenor. It should be a just cause—needs of the agency—kind of decision. Discuss the need with upper management and get their backing. Talk with the involved partner and arrange the change in a subtle and sensitive manner.

Addressing the Issue

One of the first comments you'll probably hear from the subordinate(s) confronted with a sex related matter is, "Well, it's none of your business." It is good to remember just what your business is during these confrontations. The reason *why* it is occurring may not be your business, but the fallout (*how it impacts others and the organization*) certainly is. When any act or behavior impairs, causes discomfort, inflames, or endangers others in the workplace, it becomes your business. So, it's important to keep your focus on that aspect of the situation.

When work assignments get contrived to further the agenda of either or both, or when certain displays reflect unfavorably on a professional work environment (*sexually suggestive or insensitive drawings, photos, doodling, figurines, etc*), or other acts of offensive behavior occur, then your immediate attention is required. *In today's world it doesn't matter how many enjoy the joke—it's the one who is offended and aggrieved whose interests must be addressed.*

In those situations where partners flaunt their urges by taking time off together, frequently text messaging one another, asking cohorts to cover for them or lie to a spouse or significant other, or the relationship is one sided and the recipient doesn't want the attention from the other, then it becomes your *business*—and it's time to step into the matter. *(When one officer is married or committed to another officer and becomes involved with a third—even though they conduct themselves discreetly—a potential workplace violence possibility exists.)* An important part of your role is to get things done through others. How others are impacted by the issue in terms of their safety, focus, and productivity is certainly part of that role. *A female employee complains that a male colleague brags about sexual conquests and other suggestive matters in her presence, and the colleague counter-claims that the female talks of similar lechery. Another believes an employee may be frequenting a red light district off duty, or someone else is tweeting sexually suggestive rumors about another employee, etc.* These matters must be approached with caution and delicacy.

Even if the sex related issue is off duty and/or it violates any kind of professional or legal standard, that if discovered and publicized could adversely impact the reputation of colleagues and the organization, then it is very definitely your business. So, don't let "It's none of your business" dissuade you from fulfilling your role.

Deviance

A common example is the 'Lothario Complex.' It is prevalent in men who think they are nature's gift to women and conduct themselves accordingly. Most of the time it is seen by others for what it is—comedic relief—but it can turn into seri-ous sexual harassment very quickly if left unattended. If Mr. Lothario wants to ply his misperception at home in front of the mirror, or at the lo-cal tavern off duty—that is one thing. But, it is a complex he should leave at the door when at work—period! And, NEVER pursued with regard to victims, complainants, or informants! Any hint or rumor of this happening must be immediately addressed.

In situations where erotic fantasies are being pursued during breaks, lunch hours, or away from the workplace and other employees be-come aware of it, then it may be a matter of assessing the gravity of the situation. It could range from innocuous viewing of risqué main-stream media like tabloids, GQ, or Playboy, etc., to accessing hard core pornography on personal instruments in plain view of others. The location (on premises or blatantly and carelessly public, etc.) would be a concern, along with what means (use of department re-sources) are employed to better determine its level of gravity, and if it requires official intervention.

Whatever the situation, it is an area that requires rational thought and genuine sensitivity to handle such deep-seated urges. Let professional standards help calm the storm of irrational thought and action.

What should be Done?

Regular reference to the precepts of a PWE should be woven into the normal workday communication of each manager's interaction with subordinates. Remind employees of the pitfalls of inappropriate actions, and their obligations to oath and duty and the importance of being smart—particularly with what gets sent into cyberspace.

The supervisor mentioned earlier, who would <u>frequently</u> remind em-ployees at the beginning of each shift, *"Let's remember we are here to investigate violations of federal law. Don't let anything else get in the way, etc.,"* would also add on occasion, *"Oh yeah, and don't let your glands out-maneuver your common sense, either."* It was his entertaining way of occasionally communicating the risk of allowing prurient urges to interfere with mission, and to avoid getting too chummy with suspects, victims and informants. It helped to highlight the unwholesome temptations one involved in adversarial, intimate, and sensitive work issues may encounter on occasion. Don't assume they know. Remind them every so often.

A manager should address any observation or allegation of a sexually related issue or dysfunction in a timely manner. *You overhear a female employee say to colleagues, "You guys are gross."* It may just require an off-handed comment for the guys to keep their grossness to themselves, but don't automatically discount a deeper issue in need of further counsel. Make yourself aware of departmental policy now, and approach any future matter accordingly.

You want to avoid the quagmire of stepping in between the irrational passions of two or more participants, or between the individual and his or her deviance. Stay focused on the ground that pertains to how their actions impact their job responsibilities and productivity of others. Stay tuned to the where and when, and let the professionals (counselors, etc.) deal with the why and what.

Also, be ready to diffuse disdain, bemusement, or light heartedness (joking) about sexual matters by others. This is especially true today with the increasing visibility and acceptance of alternative lifestyles and any lingering resistance to gay, lesbian, or trans-gender situations.

When it is a relatively minor or nebulous matter (true intent veiled with double meaning), merely taking the person aside and telling them to stop what they're doing in the work setting is sufficient to resolve the matter. *A dispatcher uses voice inflection and innuendo to imply a sexual connotation to a message being transmitted to an officer he or she may be involved with. "Roger on that spelling, is it O—as in Oral?" (emphasis added.)* He or she will likely give you a blank stare like they don't know what you're talking about, and may deny the true intent, but will likely stop if told to do so.

However, if it involves a complicated issue, or an employee who doesn't respond well to your directions, include another supervisor as a witness. Document whatever action you take to deal with the situation. It is highly recommended that complainants, suspects, and victims of the opposite sex are addressed by two officers wherever possible—including informants.

If one or both partners are married or otherwise encumbered, then steps should be taken to lessen their access to one another during working hours. Any organization is fully justified in readjusting the situation without acrimony or defensiveness. Counseling about responsibilities to family and organization may help to wake them up out of their blissful irrationality, or a referral to an appropriate in-house remedy may be warranted.

Don't get lurid in details. Avoid judging or discussing the details of the acts or interrelationships, and only deal with how their actions impact peers and the organization. However, be ready to give substantive reasons for your concern to articulate exactly why you are addressing the issue and making the necessary change.

Be sure to look at the issue from all perspectives. *The person claiming unwanted attention from another has text messaged the other with flirtatious or suggestive content.* It is important to weigh equally each participant's input to avoid favoring one over the other based on gender or sexual orientation. If there are genuine mitigating circumstances, then include them in your assessment of the issue.

Hopefully your organization has written policies and guidelines on personal relationships. Policies should include management's right to reassign personnel according to agency needs. Policies should include counseling that is available to afford those involved the opportunity to see their way through both the organization's and *their* own self interests. Properly proposed and facilitated, changes made should be to the satisfaction of everyone—especially the paramours.

Off duty relationships or activities should be addressed only as they relate to any potential violation of local ordinances and state laws as in public indecency, prostitution, bigamy, statutory rape, etc. And, if there is no such policy, then, as a manager/leader, you should suggest the organization create one. It would certainly help to keep your work environment **professional**.

Bottom line—deal with it; don't let it fester. Action taken at the out-set can often ward off a more complicated situation the longer it is allowed to evolve.

CHAPTER 16

Discrimination

Discrimination is all about choice and preference. Everyone chooses. We prefer certain things over others (food, cars, sports teams, hair color, clothes; the list goes on and on). The term gets ugly when an individual or group places another individual or group in an uncomfortable position or at a disadvantage based on *who they are or what they may be*.

From race and gender to sexual orientation and beyond, it basically involves the few, the different, and now legally protected category being absorbed, accommodated, and accepted by all employees you are managing. It is an imbalance that must be evened out, made smooth, and maintained.

There are laws that define discrimination, but it's one's actions that drive it. Actions that discriminate come from preferential thoughts, whether you are conscious of them or not. *It's wise to consider discrimination in <u>any</u> form, whether defined or not, as probably wrong.* Besides, who knows when something not defined by law becomes the next legal challenge management must face? (Short versus tall, fat and skinny, smart or less so, etc.)

That's because …

None of us have any choice in *who* we are as human beings. We are who we are due to the reality of nature itself. Race, ethnicity, national origin, gender, and age are determined by circumstances beyond anyone's control. (*No one chooses to be handicapped or grow old*). How one evolves socially out of that mix should have no bearing on how he or she is managed. So, to allow others as part of a majority to exclude, antagonize, discomfort or restrict another based on a prejudicial preference is just plain wrong—Period! Not only does it violate laws that now protect certain classifications of people, but the very basis of the constitutional mandate you have <u>solemnly</u> sworn to uphold which declares <u>everyone</u> is equal in the eyes of the law. Your role as a manager is to do what you can to make sure that happens.

Anything that seems to single out or make uncomfortable *any* kind of minority in a majority setting is something a manager must constantly be on guard for. *It could be a look, a word, an innuendo, a gesture, or any number or combination of actions that show up anywhere in any form—the bulletin board, tweets, a picture on a desk, an offhanded comment, a joke, or action by another or others.* It can be how *you*—the manager—distribute resources, assign duty, etc. It covers a lot of ground, so it is important to have this concept firmly planted in the back of your mind, and never let the status quo or majority preference overrule your obligation to manage equally according to your role as a manager.

You may not like an employee as much as the others, or feel awkward or disinclined to interact with him or her. But, much of management is looking beyond what is traditional and comfortable and engaging that which is more relevant and necessary for the sake of the mission and your role.

Also, don't forget discrimination is a claim that *anyone* can stake. It may not be the offended making the claim. (A family member or friend of an aggrieved employee reports the issue.) In some states, managers can be held personally responsible for acts of discrimination they commit themselves. It is a minefield of potential problems for those who allow it to exist.

What to do

Be AWARE! Try to truly understand the other's perspective. (Investigators do that all the time). Try to see what someone with protected status would see if you were in their position. When some*one* is *one* of many, there are sensitivities that must be understood and accommodated. *A lone female in a majority male setting will consciously sense the uniqueness of her situation. She will be aware of and more sensitive to any kind of difference, i.e., exclusion, resistance or favoritism, as the lone male would naturally sense in a majority female setting.*

Keep it in the back of your mind while carrying out your responsibilities. (What you and <u>others</u> say and do, and especially how you assign, evaluate, and interact with <u>everyone</u>.) It is important to keep a discriminating symptom from becoming a pattern of activity.

You may hear an employee make a crude racial or ethnic comment to another who may laugh and seem not to be offended. *The group seems comfortable with jabbing each other's ethnicity, race, or gender.* You should address this seemingly innocuous exchange with the instigator and/or the recipient immediately. Try to determine if there is any sensitivity to what transpired. Tell them not to do it, and it just may stop. With a crude or insensitive joke, it's not about how many laugh, but who doesn't that must be the concern. If that is the case—then do something about it. Don't let it fester. <u>Go out of your way to be inclusive.</u>

Talk to people whether they are subordinates, peers, or even superiors. Remember, it should not happen in a PWE. The offhanded comment, "Screw these people," uttered in the midst of frustration should be addressed sooner rather than later. *The female employee laughingly says, "You guys are disgusting."* An anonymous caller alleges discrimination by one of your employees. Don't discount or ignore the call just because it is anonymous. Follow up. Look into it. Determine if it is something that merits closer and more official attention.

If unprofessional behavior persists despite your initial efforts, then address it more formally in terms of documenting your efforts. Don't try to alleviate the situation by thinking you are helping an offend**ed** by moving them to another location or assignment. Think more in terms of moving the offend**er** (cause) of the issue.

CHAPTER 17

Informants

Informants are people recruited—and sometimes coerced—into providing information for intelligence and/or criminal investigative purposes, but whose identity must remain confidential and protected from disclosure. From the taint of corruption if lured or entangled in inappropriate or criminal activity, to the mechanics of how the informant is operated and the veracity of the information obtained, the use of informants is incredibly unpredictable and involves great risk.

It is an unconventional and often dysfunctional domain of interpersonal relationships between law enforcement and <u>anyone</u> in a position to provide needed information. <u>No other field of endeavor has such a unique and controversial brand.</u>

It is a surreptitious realm where discipline, rules, and responsibility for enforcing the law must indulge devious human behavior, or accommodate and sometimes participate in criminality for the sake of achieving a <u>greater good</u>. It can be a very dangerous area of endeavor, too.

The constant in the uncertainty of this unique area is the need for identity protection while producing information for operational use and probable disclosure. It is a balance that requires <u>good judgment</u> on the part of those operating (handling) the informant and the manager responsible for its oversight.

As for managing employees engaging informants, especially those to be used on a <u>continuous basis</u>, it is important for supervisors to have a few key concerns firmly planted in mind.

Its Personal

The top concern for a supervisor should be that while the employee (handler) is 'working' his or her informant, <u>it is highly probable the informant is trying to 'work' (compromise) the handler, too</u>. Few informants provide information out of the goodness of their hearts. The stigma of informing is a difficult barrier for anyone of any culture to overcome and maintain.

There is usually a subtle, if not direct expectation by the informant that whatever he or she gives to the handler, the handler will recompense in some way, too. While the handler may be ignoring what the informant is doing illegally, helping them with some pending official action, giving them money, etc., there is always the risk the informant will try to balance the relationship with offers of sex, picking up a tab, facilitating a personal matter, to bribery and beyond.

The handler (your subordinate), on the other hand, can fall victim to an unrealistic sense of ownership regarding the informant. *There are some cases where the handler and informant truly come to like each other, where the bond of friendship and loyalty compete with honesty and professional responsibility.* The handler may feel that the importance of this surreptitious relationship he or she worked hard to develop deserves accommodation and/or privilege beyond what is reasonably or legally allowable. Be careful of handler's filtering information from informant. (This can happen when the Handler purposely fails to report information that is derogatory about or injurious to the informant to protect his or her continued use).

Meanwhile, management can acquire an unrealistic view that verbal orders, written directives and agreements will control an informant's behavior throughout the relationship, and hold the handler accountable accordingly.

Be very <u>wary</u> of the relationship aspect of this kind of endeavor, for there dwells the greatest hazard—the draw of unanticipated affinity and/or intimacy as it evolves. The handling subordinate must be regularly reminded, and the supervisor always aware that a gap must be maintained (an interpersonal distance). It requires a degree of wariness, vigilance, and attention unlike any other kind of relationship. It must remain strictly professional, i.e., your employee is the handler and the informant informs. It should never be a two way street—*I do this for you—you do this for me*—<u>unless officially authorized</u>.

<u>Be very careful of what is promised.</u> (Assume the informant could be recording you). Keeping an informant's identity protected can no longer be guaranteed. If the informant has any information favorable to a defendant who has requested it (Brady v. Maryland, 1963), or has been promised not to be prosecuted in exchange for testimony (Giglio v. United States, 1972), it is legally required for the prosecution to furnish it to the defense. Under certain of those circumstances, the informant may be forced to testify. *To avoid civil liability that could occur if an informant loses his or her job, is physically assaulted, or further retaliated against for informing, it is imperative for the a supervisor to ensure the informant's file is documented that the informant understands that his or her identity may surface if called as a witness.* This is an extremely high risk component for working informants. Handlers have to be properly trained to delicately explain this to their informants.

The bottom line is that informants are not friends, cohorts, or those whose plight or perceived importance deserves anything other than what is rationally and legally defensible and officially sanctioned.

The Informant's Purpose

Law enforcement agencies engage informants to acquire information that serves a necessary investigative or intelligence gathering purpose (greater good). The more accurate and informative the information provided, the more likely the informant is closely associated with or engaged in the kind of criminality being revealed. It is absolutely essential they remain the lesser players in the goal or higher purpose of the agency's investigative or intelligence gathering efforts. *An active burglar providing information on other burglars would be hard to justify to a jury or prosecutor. However, the same burglar (if his or her criminal activity is curbed during the relationship) providing information on gang activity, organized crime or terrorism would be more acceptable.*

The Problem

At what point does the relationship become something where the handler and/or the informant's behavior begins to adversely impact the value and legitimacy of the information produced?

Informants seldom give up all their information, anyway. They often minimize what they know for future leverage and/or personal gain. While an informant may be involved in lesser crimes—*booking numbers, being a lookout for a drug gang, laundering money, receiving stolen goods, taking kick backs, an elected official's aide is the "bagman" in a political corruption case, etc., etc.,*—the informant should be moving the handler *up* the ladder of priority in order to resolve more heinous crimes or larger, longer term crime problems or intelligence goals.

It is also very important for informants to cease, or at least limit, whatever criminality they engage in for the duration of any official Handler/Informant relationship. *The informant owns a local bar known to receive stolen goods, serve minors on occasion or allow prostitution on premises, etc., but provides valuable information on gang activity, organized crime, homicides, and other major crimes. The informant derives the information from the criminals he or she interacts with through the ancillary criminal activities that go on at the bar.*

It will fall on the supervisor to assess the gravity of the circumstances (the risk of injury to innocent third parties), versus the activity to be ignored or tolerated that enables the informant to continue operating as usual. *(As in the bar owner, the risk of an underage patron being involved in a serious accident, etc).*

Be prepared to justify this relationship with a clear understanding and articulation on how it serves a more important and valuable purpose.

Remember, having knowledge of an informant's criminality— and doing nothing—inadvertently sanctions that activity, and can absorb you <u>and</u> the organization into its culpability.

So, how does one deal with what has been a productive relationship, but suspicion or revelation of unacceptable activity comes to light? *You begin to suspect your numbers runner is actually an enforcer—beating, even killing people. The lookout is actually dealing, and the guy taking kickbacks is embezzling larger sums than previously thought. The aide to the politician may be deep into child pornography or molestation, or the owner of the bar may be the ringleader of a vicious robbery ring, etc., etc.* At what point does the informant's suspected, newly discovered, or known unauthorized criminal activity begin to outweigh the benefit of the information he or she provides?

Do you make an effort to resolve it at the risk of losing a valuable resource? Where do you draw the line that means losing, even charging the informant with a crime? The handler may have accommodated the informant, looked the other way on occasion, but now there is a growing concern the informant may be duping the handler, or is risking the integrity of the investigative effort. It is a very murky realm, which will challenge everyone's judgmental competency to the hilt! In other words, the higher the risk the more critical the goal should be.

Prevention

BEWARE the subtle indicators of probable trouble:

- The handler seems to over value the informant, or is overly sensitive to questions about or criticism of the informant.

- You sense too much fraternization between handler and informant.

- You may suspect the handler is filtering information from the informant.

- Be wary of time expended by the handler versus too little production from the informant.

- Take seriously any concerns raised by colleagues concerning the relationship.

Any and all of these may indicate the professional relationship is getting out of sync—that the handler may be "handling" beyond professional bounds. Don't extend the benefit of the doubt too much in this kind of relationship. Stay true to your instinct, and question whatever uncertainty you feel. Clear and honest assessment must prevail throughout.

The Process

Written guidelines for informants are good to have. The more information on record regarding the relationship, the better it helps protect not only the safety of and integrity of the handler, but the veracity of information obtained, too.

There *should* be a confidential administrative process to address all aspects of informant utilization, including their biographical and contact information. *This helps protect the handler should something go terribly wrong (a need to identify and access informant absent the availability of the handler).* The informant's identity can be disguised by code names or numbers and kept separate from the information provided. It should be kept in a secure place and inaccessible to other employees.

Any significant transgression or unapproved activity should be on record, too—especially any that need *fixing* in order to continue the informant's use for critically important matters. Because an informant surprised the handler with unanticipated criminal activity (*was in a fight, caught shoplifting, arrested for DUI, domestic abuse, etc.*) doesn't necessarily preclude his or her continued use. It will depend on the gravity of the circumstance weighed against the importance of the informant's access to information needed to accomplish the investigative goal.

The manager and officiating overseers (ranking officers, prosecutor, etc.) must be the judge of that and not left up to the handler.

Informant information to be disclosed in reports and affidavits should be reviewed to ensure the informant's identity is sufficiently disguised from deductive reasoning. *Instead of "every Tuesday informant was in a position to observe the exchange," it would be best to say, "On at least two occasions informant was in a position to see the exchange."* Observing the exchange is important. The where, when, or how can be adjusted to protect the informant's identity depending upon the circumstances when prepping the information for disclosure.

Electronic or email exchanges with informants are a treasure trove for discovery, and should be prohibited, or at least minimized and properly disguised, to protect his or her identity and activity.

The Need for Transparency?

While transparency in a surreptitious realm sounds like a contradiction—it's not. Candor and openness definitely have a place in this process.

There must be transparency *with* the <u>informant</u> to the extent he or she is aware of the handler's bottom line—up front: no gifts, favors, or activity (social or criminal) outside what is appropriate and officially sanctioned. A record of this proffer should be part of the file. Be very careful of what is promised. Remember, no one can promise absolute confidentiality. In addition, always assume your interactions with the informant may be recorded by him or her in some fashion.

There must be transparency *with* <u>you—the supervisor</u>—to the extent the handler keeps you informed of not only the information being provided (both helpful *and* harmful), but how (mechanics) he or she is handling the informant to ensure the relationship doesn't drift into inappropriate territory.

Create and maintain a regularly scheduled review process to assess suitability, productivity, and the integrity of the relationship between the handler and informant, and the information being provided. If you sense an inappropriate drift in the relationship, then immediately coach the handler back into focus and propriety with regular follow up, or sever the relationship if necessary.

CHAPTER 18

Social Media

If there were ever a cyber world *golden rule* for personal use of social media, it would probably be *"The less work related posting the better."*

Social media has become one of the most precarious areas of endeavor for an organization and its employees to handle. While it can be a helpful investigative and operational tool, it is the personal use that will probably concern first line managers the most. *It's like leaving roll call and going out on patrol, where the shift supervisor's admonition to "Be Careful Out There" really comes home to roost.* Many departments already have rules pertaining to media use by employees. However, it will still fall on the first line manager to help avert misuse by maintaining subordinate awareness of its perils through coaching and counseling accordingly.

Law enforcement is a very unique and sensitive position to hold in our society. Its very nature can have one person's indiscretion reflecting on so many others and sometimes the entire profession—like it or not. There are countless unanticipated risks that can impact you and others in ways never imagined. No matter how proud one is of a position in law enforcement, one should refrain from posting your status or any stories or experiences in the law enforcement realm on any personal social media platform.

Once you've identified yourself as a law enforcer, certain public expectations can attach to your online persona. Your actions take on greater meaning not just to yourself, but to your professional responsibilities, peers, and the organization as well. *An innocently intended sarcastic or satirical comment you assume peers and known friends will understand and enjoy could be interpreted as biased, bigoted, or discriminatory by others not intended as recipients, and—in turn—passed on to an untold number of others.*

The key is to be professional, not emotional. Nothing confidential, sensitive, or revealing about any duty or action in an official capacity should get posted <u>anywhere</u>. While there are many poignant and humorous human interest stories that are often shared with peers during peer interactions and social gatherings—<u>they should stay private.</u> *Going viral can be a shocking phenomenon. It can turn what was intended for a local or limited audience into a nationwide headline issue.* Anything one feels would have positive public relations benefit should be first reviewed and authorized by the head of the organization.

From U-tube, Facebook, Twitter and blogging, to Instagram, hashtagging and whatever lies beyond, legal challenges surrounding free speech and its impact on an employer's operational and personnel issues will continue to be sorted out in the courts and tough to manage for the foreseeable future. *Under certain circumstances, opinions and comments critical of supervisors and the organization are protected speech.* It is important to remember that *anyone* can access your postings, including criminals, defense attorneys, activists, terrorists—all of which can have unforeseen, negative consequences for the posting employee, his or her peers, *and* the organization.

The importance for law enforcers to maintain the public trust by being apolitical (neutral) in their public persona also extends to how they conduct themselves in private, as well. It is not so much a matter of suppressing free speech as it is making sure what is said and done on line is impartial, mature, and professional for the purpose of maintaining trust. It's possible *any* kind of posting could be used against you in court or hinder future career choices (for example, sensitive or undercover matters). The list of hazards goes on and on. *Even anonymously clicking one button in support of a controversial or potentially sensitive issue can have a deleterious impact on many others.*

If you must post, make sure it is factual and provable. It is a permanent record. *Posting or publishing anything in response to or critical of a law enforcement related event should be through more formal and professional outlets. That would include a letter to the editor, an Op Ed piece, or a reputable nationally recognized blogging or web site—places where comments are vetted or at least shared on a professional platform.*

Don't let emotion compel a posting you later wish you hadn't. (*A nationally publicized violent demonstration decrying police practices was further aggravated by an unassociated officer's unprofessional rant on line about the demonstrators. The officer may face punishment by his employer for doing it, but the damage to law enforcement was already done*).

Don't place yourself in a position to answer questions from lurkers or friends on official policy. Avoid inadvertently competing with your organization. It's not that you can't, but more that you *should not* engage in any sensitive (sexual orientation, race, ethnicity, etc.) matter that could morph you into a quasi-official source to those who can't distinguish between personal opinion and professional position.

In very simple terms, it is a matter of being smart versus foolish. And that means never letting emotion dictate what you feel compelled to post online. Exercise caution. Use common sense. Steer clear of controversy online.

WHAT TO DO AS A SUPERVISOR

Don't forget to explore *your* attitude toward and use of social media. Are you in line with your department's on line policy? Don't engage in activity you would not want your employees to do.

It will not be your responsibility to monitor an employee's personal use of social media. However, when you learn of an impropriety, it will require an intervention—at least to the extent the employee is counseled and coached regarding proper and expected use.

It *is* your role however, to foresee the potential risks as social media innovations evolve, and to coach your subordinates accordingly. *Social media sites are in a state of constant flux and will continue to be so for the foreseeable future.*

Listen to your subordinates. *It is hard to scoff at any issue these days.* Try to head off potential problems that could end up on social media outlets. Don't avoid disgruntled employees. Talk to them. Encourage employees to bring issues to you first and avoid venting online—even to friends and peers. Make sure everyone has a legitimate avenue to vent frustrations or complaints.

Occasionally train employees on social media use. Don't just regurgitate existing policy requirements; focus on the reasoning behind the requirements. Educate employees on the potential risks and ramifications and what is not protected—offensive language, harassment, disparagement of other employees, discriminatory statements, sexual innuendo, inappropriate statements about religion, etc.

Everyone should reread their postings from a third person perspective to ensure they will not be exhibiting or implying any kind of discrimination, insensitive levity, or inappropriate decorum in anything they are posting. Consider how it could be perceived by the average citizen.

As a supervisor, always keep in mind the fundamental principle of fairness. Not all employees will engage in social media in the same way. Be careful of the implication if you interact on line with some to the exclusion of others. As a supervisor, you shouldn't *friend* subordinates, or seek their connection, or respond in kind. Even if you keep such actions neutral or innocuous, it may reflect an image of being unfair to others who don't participate in kind.

Never coach, counsel, or admonish employees on line.

Any training or information imparted to employees about their use of social media should be documented.

CHAPTER 19

Whistle Blowers

An employee approaches you with information that certain other officers and their supervisor are extorting a local business owner. One of the alleged offenders is a friend.

Whistle blowers (WB) are people who raise seemingly valid, yet sometimes unproven, allegations involving potentially serious consequences. They present a challenge for those first to hear of the allegations, or who must manage them during the upheaval their pending claims create.

Most states have adopted laws that mirror federal efforts to protect whistle blowers from retaliation. There are private watch dog organizations, which can take up the cause of an aggrieved whistle blower, and the media revels in these cases as well. So, it is important for the manager first hearing the allegation or managing an aggrieved WB to proceed in a manner that protects both the WB *and* the integrity of the organization apart from what is being revealed or alleged.

In some cases WBs raise issues of wrongdoing that others may have suspected through rumor or innuendo, but never wanted to believe or had ignored, and may feel the WB is *upsetting the apple cart*. Just the title, Whistle Blower, has a negative connotation in our culture. They compete against a culturally ingrained undertone of aversion for those who tell on others. So, it is somewhat understandable how the emotional reaction of others (not involved) would drift toward the messenger (WB) rather than the actual cause of the dysfunction or illegality alleged.

Whether the WB's claims are valid or not, *WBs only need to reasonably believe the issue is occurring. If proven wrong they are still protected under law.* Management's response is key to how the controversy plays out regarding its appropriate resolution and ensuing public perception and trust. As seen in many controversies, it's not so much the original sin, but how people react to it that compounds the ultimate outcome. It can place the WB's immediate supervisor in a real quandary, especially if the claims involve superiors or cohorts you know. *If it involves a superior, and you're unsure of the risk of reporting it through normal channels, you might have to direct or help the WB connect to a trusted level above the suspected official, or to a more secure alternate channel. This as opposed to ignoring the allegation, or carelessly disclosing the WB's identity and claim prior to its validation.* It could fuel a conflict between honesty, loyalty, and friendship, in ways hard to imagine. It could test the very core of your character. It's important to remember: <u>If the allegations are true, it is the wrongdoer who is upsetting the apple cart—not the WB</u>.

If you are managing a WB who has garnered the wrath of peers and higher rank because of their previous complaint or unsettling disclosure, it places you in a difficult position. You have to manage him or her based strictly on performance, and not in relation to what they've done, how you feel personally, or what others think you should do. You want to avoid any hint of retaliation. The final resolution of the WB's status will be out of your domain anyway, but your involvement (however temporary or superficial) could play a larger part than you realize in later efforts to adjudicate the issue.

CHAPTER 20

Accountability

(Evaluating others)

Bottom Line: employees are paid <u>to do</u> something—engage in activity—to perform. What they <u>do</u> must support the organization's mission, goals and objectives, and conform to its rules and regulations within the law. However, it is important to note, while management may influence one's inclination to engage in activity one way or the other, <u>it is the employee</u> who will ultimately determine to what extent and manner he or she will engage in such activity.

Evaluating subordinates will be one of the most challenging and important endeavors engaged in by a supervisor. Too many managers approach this responsibility with reluctance and uncertainty. Some are wary of the time and effort needed to do it, the potential for conflict, and a misperceived negativity toward documenting others. However, this supervisory responsibility lies at the heart of *how* organizations know what is being done is getting done as expected.

Responsibility and Expectation are key words in this realm. Responsibility is something you should do because it is morally right or legally required. Everyone is responsible for and to something or someone. However, underlying responsibility is <u>expectation</u>—the 'how' one does, as expected, by what or those they are responsible to or for.

Responsibility in our private lives is driven by social norms and common or enacted laws that serve as ground rules for socially preferred and expected behavior. *How one fulfills their responsibility influences the perception of others as to how they measure-up as a husband, wife, father or mother, friend or associate, citizen and neighbor, etc., etc.*

Workplace responsibility is more formalized with mission, goals, objectives, and their ensuing rules, regulations and the cultural norms that frame an employer's expectations for employee activity while on the job. *An important supervisory responsibility is to evaluate subordinate performance. The organization expects it.*

Therein lies accountability: assessing employee activity for the law enforcement organization to ensure proper use of time, authority, and public resources. Are employees doing what's expected not just by the organization, but the public, too? **Responsibility** outlines what has to be done. **Expectation** influences how it will be done. **Accountability** attends to how it's actually getting done.

All these concepts get massaged into formal instruments designed for assessing employee behavior and productivity commonly known as performance evaluations or appraisals.

Performance Evaluation

Performance has to do with an activity engaged in and the result produced. The quality of human interaction is such an important part of law enforcement productivity that agencies must look beyond statistics and address the *effect* of employee actions behind those numbers. Counting traffic stops and citations, response time, written reports produced, cases closed, etc., will not determine or reflect overall success of the agency's mission. *A citizen asking for directions is flippantly told by the officer to "keep walking, you'll see it." The directions may have sufficed, but the action engaged in by the officer probably undermined the quality of service rendered.* In other words, try not to confuse numbers with accomplishment or success.

Performance evaluations serve two important purposes. One is to regularly convey employer expectations to employees, and the other is to provide a range of measures for managers to assess and employees to know what they must do to meet them. All kinds of behavioral factors, i.e., dependability, initiative, leadership, communication, competency are identified as measures to address the quality of an employee's performance, which can sometimes be ambiguous.

Counting tangible results (quantity) is easy. Accounting (ensuring quality of quantity) requires greater analysis and effort.

So while performance evaluations may have differing formats, they all serve a single purpose—to assess the *quality* of employee actions and effort, which includes the quantity of what he or she produces.

Everyone Does Not Perform the Same

A backdrop to this hodgepodge of terms and concepts is the importance of **fairness**. Standards and expectations must be reasonable and proper. Holding people accountable for what they've done or failed to do must be fair and impartial. Some employees are smarter than others, more organized, better interviewers, informant handlers, writers, speakers, etc. *Regardless of how employees are grouped by generational labels, i.e., Gen X or Y-ers, boomers, millenials, etc., each must possess common interpersonal qualities to be effective in the law enforcement realm.*

There are production variances, too. There are cases developed versus the ones assigned, the harder one unsolved versus the easy one closed, and the prodigious ticket writer outpacing those who use better discretion? There are some who exceed expectations, but in a manner that upsets group equilibrium and team dynamics.

There are broader, more esoteric issues to be considered. The more one does the greater the likelihood of mistake versus the one who plays it safe all the time. There is a tough line to be drawn between encouraging risk and experimentation, and then holding one accountable when they fail or overdo what was intended. Is the organization under stress, investigation, facing prolonged social unrest, or having disaster related issues?

Bottom Line, the best way to ensure fairness is to make sure employees are assessed <u>individually</u> according to established standards and measures. *The outstanding employee is not valid to use as a comparison standard, just as an unsatisfactory employee is not to be used in a similar fashion.* Supervisors must consider these and other intangibles and fit them into their assessments according to established evaluation standards and categories.

Narrative is an important part of this capability, and it requires good documentation. It's great when the employee agrees with your assessment. However, when there is a gap between what you assess and what the employee believes his or her output to be, documentation will narrow the difference.

Documentation

It's NOT "keeping book" as it is sometimes perceived by subordinates—a nasty term that implies subterfuge and distrust. Secrecy helps foster that kind of perception.

All law enforcers document; enforcing the law involves constant documentation. It sits at the core of their job requirements, whether writing a citation, recording an interview, doing an investigation, reporting suspicious activity, or accounting for daily and/or hourly activity. It's possible that this kind of documentation, most of which is to support potential prosecution, intelligence, or for organizational control, could undermine the concept when it comes to subordinate performance.

The newly promoted supervisor has to move beyond any nuanced negativity, and see it for what it really is—<u>an important and effective management tool for recognizing good performance *and/or* identifying deficiencies both of which are important for accounting and improving performance.</u>

In order to avoid a negative connotation like "keeping book," performance documentation must be transparent—shared with the employee during reviews. Its purpose must be discussed with the subordinate as a positive effort for recognizing good performance or identifying areas in need of improvement.

Documentation must be accumulated the same way for everyone and used for assessing performance only. The physical or electronic file must accommodate all kinds of documentation from notes of observation, a copy of a written report, social media postings, email, photos, etc., to citations, unique accomplishments, accolades, and beyond. Include all materials that apply to the established measurable standards.

It bolsters the feedback subordinates need to have as they fulfill their job responsibilities. It helps narrow the gap between what they may see as their performance, and what you and facts determine to be otherwise.

How Best to Hold Others Accountable

Accountability begins with fully accepting *your* responsibility for appraising subordinate performance. Get to know and believe performance evaluation is an important management tool. This may mean adjusting *your* frame of mind regarding performance evaluation and how you hold yourself accountable, as well.

A previous mentor valued employees on the basis of how well he or she did what they DIDN'T like to do. His premise was based on an assumption that everyone did well what they liked to do. Prima donnas only did what they liked to do, but it was those who did everything well—especially that which they didn't like to do—who were valued most of all. The same premise could apply to a manager's approach to performance evaluation as well.

Discuss the organizational value of performance evaluation with subordinates during their appraisals. Tell them—up front—that you consider it an important part of their responsibility as well as yours. There's nothing wrong with an employee bringing something to your attention that could help you with their evaluation. Engage employees in providing documentation. Allow them to express or share their success on occasion, or ask for help if needed. *For example, an employee is unsure of how to write an affidavit, and they ask for your help. Their request for help could be considered a positive action to be documented as such in support of a behavioral standard like "Initiative," etc.*

If you truly believe in the importance of evaluation and approach it as it was meant to be, subordinates will eventually believe it, too. *The organization can have the best engineered performance appraisal on the market, but if you aren't there in spirit and intent it won't be as effective as it needs to be.*

The semi and/or annual performance write-up is only one part of what should be a continuing process throughout the rating period.

Accountability should include timely and routine documentation and feedback. Even in agencies with no formal evaluations, tell employees how they are doing _when_ they are doing it. Once yearly is not enough. _Effective coaches are constantly aware of both proficiency and deficiency and look for ways (using imagination and ingenuity) to effectively recognize or improve employee performance._

Performance documentation and evaluation takes time, so it will be important to make time to do it. Span of control and operational demand may impact your ability to live up to what is required, but the responsibility will not be any less, regardless of the size, location, or situation. _It is one thing to be responsible for a few versus many, or for employees who are working at home or are dispersed geographically._ Like those who keep diaries, it may mean taking time at the end of a hectic day to record observations regarding employee performance while still fresh in mind.

There must be an effort to meet face to face with scattered or hard to access employees frequently enough to observe their activity and interaction with others (clients, public, etc.) to better assess _how_ they are accomplishing their productivity.

Be careful of performance inflation—elevating employees above their actual ability to avoid confrontation. _Employees will naturally want high ratings while employers may pressure for lower scores._ Tell it like it is, and be able to back it up.

The main thrust of your effort should be to improve productivity as well as deficiencies—not to punish. Any effort made to help an employee improve performance before initiating any progressive discipline only bolsters a manager's position. This is especially true when dealing with those who consciously choose to engage in activity at odds with the employer's expectations.

Remember the expectation of courage in fulfilling your role—to do what is right, regardless of the circumstances or consequences.

CHAPTER 21

Crime Scenes
(First Supervisor There)

As a first line supervisor, you'll probably be the first of management at the scene. The tape is going up, cars are responding, and the scene is a hodgepodge of people. It's time to assert yourself.

Even though subordinates may be well versed in processing a crime scene, don't delegate the responsibility entirely. The overall symmetry and organization is your responsibility. Your job is to assign personnel appropriately, coordinate their activities, and be available for guidance and decision making. *It is important to remember—what has to get done functionally will be done by others (subordinates).*

For first line supervisors, crime scenes can be divided into three categories—Passive, Active, and Employee Involved.

A Passive Scene

In a Passive scenario, you have the luxury of a dormant scene. *The offender is gone and there is no further threat or danger to responding personnel.* The integrity of the scene becomes paramount. The scene must be secured and access strictly controlled and accounted for, so crime scene specialists and assigned investigators can do their job without undue interference and contamination.

Area interviews, surrounding search sites, and other ancillary responsibilities must be arranged and assigned, and the results passed through a central point where information and evidence obtained can be recorded and entered into a chain of custody. *Remember to take notes as they relate to your actions in maintaining the integrity and proficiency of the scene.*

The Active Scene

In the **Active** scenario, your first concerns will center on trying to get the upper hand over what could be a very chaotic and dangerous situation. Like fighting a fire, one must determine the kind of fire you face to apply the proper resources strategically and keep it from spreading.

Active scenes are ongoing and potentially expansive. *The crime may continue to unfold with increasing numbers of victims or offenders discovered, with further destruction possible, and/or a likelihood of it spilling into other areas.* Active will inevitably involve a superior rank and/or a specialty soon taking control. But, in the interim, you're in charge.

As the first arriving supervisor your initial concerns will depend on what you have and need in resources to strategically address the situation you face. From large area crime scenes like an aircraft crashing from the sky, armed assault at a school or mall, a fiery explosion, or hazardous materials, to a sniping from an unknown or superior vantage point, a hostage taking, and beyond—don't wait around for higher rank. Take command of the situation.

Consider perimeter security, communication, personnel placement to protect innocent lives, close off or limit possible offender escape routes, intelligence gathering, and directing to safe haven those fleeing to determine what you have (how many offenders, where they are, who is trapped, existence of hazardous materials, etc). These will become your paramount concerns. How will you utilize personnel in a strategic manner? Crowd control could be a priority concern.

In situations where immediate interdiction may seem necessary, (*you hear or believe more victims are at imminent risk*), try to remain professional and do not get emotional. *In today's international and domestic terrorist threat, there is the potential for responder-directed scenarios that may require more caution than courage.* The possibility of being drawn into an ambush or falling victim to remote controlled devices, drones, and/or secondary explosions, etc., should be a real concern of the responding supervisor.

Remember, the overall symmetry and organization of the scene will be your responsibility. *It's time to think and plan and not react emotionally. Prioritize needs with what you have in resources.*

Consider locating a command and control setting and/or staging area to accommodate responding personnel and vehicles close enough to the scene, yet far enough away to ensure the control center's unimpeded safety and operation. Advertise its existence and location, and then make sure personnel report to you on what they are doing, and any information they obtain. This will help you to brief arriving higher rank and specialties (fire departments, SWAT, state or federal agencies, etc.).

Also, you must be aware of the time and record significant events and situations as they occur, or as soon after as possible. Remember, even chaotic scenes will one day become evidence in court.

Employee Involved (E-I) Crime Scenes

When an employee recklessly or willfully engages in criminal activity, or even questionable misconduct, one could assume they would forfeit any expectation of loyalty or friendship from peers or cohorts. But, that's not always the case. There are interpersonal intangibles that make an E-I investigation different. Years of familiarity, camaraderie, deference to loyalty and friendship, and sense of entitlement can inadvertently mitigate an E-I's actions. The need for a supervisor to remain impartial yet supportive to the extent it doesn't interfere with the integrity of the investigation and resolution will be a delicate part of the mix.

Naturally, as a supervisor, you would ensure the E-I is afforded the due process he or she is entitled to under the law, and be honest and forthright about official policy and procedures. It's not just the crime, but the potential for civil action, too, that requires an unassailable collection and assessment of evidence and investigative follow through. However, it is the reality of today's management responsibility to accommodate employee sensitivities and welfare, even when under suspicion or accused of misconduct or a crime.

Interaction with the E-I should include as much empathy and benefit of doubt as can be reasonably afforded throughout the ordeal and its aftermath. Remember, other personnel will be watching. *One of the most disconcerting experiences for anyone suspected of a crime and not yet fully adjudicated is the accusatory, contemptuous, and isolationist stance assumed by some personnel—especially management.* Any kind of similar approach by management can be seen by other subordinates as lacking the respect and benefit of doubt they feel a fellow employee deserves professionally. It can unsettle group cohesiveness long after the issue is resolved—regardless of the E-I's guilt or innocence. In other words, until the facts are sorted and an official position is taken (suspension, arrest, termination, etc.) it is a matter of doing what has to be done in a humane and respectful, yet impartial manner.

However, a supervisor must also be wary of any E-I efforts to garner undeserved sympathy or help from peers relating to his or her situation. Any effort to intercede on behalf of the E-I should be monitored to ensure the integrity of the process and resolution. A continuing effort must be made to avoid a drift of loyalty and friendship into inappropriate territory.

If assigned an E-I while his or her issue is pending, and you have no official interest except to manage the interim assignment, be sure to assess performance strictly on how the E-I meets departmental evaluation standards in real time. Don't let past actions, reputation, or likely outcome influence your judgment. Don't avoid or isolate the E-I. Try to interact normally during his or her time in limbo. The specifics of an E-I's dilemma should not be the concern of other personnel, so do what you can to keep it that way.

Address any rumors, meddling, or undeserved sentiments as soon as you become aware of it. Remain aware of and try to be empathetic to stressors impacting the E-I during his or her time assigned to you. Take time to listen to his or her concerns or fears. Be wary of your own prejudgment. It will influence the tenor of your interaction with the E-I and how it is seen by others. Suspicion can linger, even if the E-I is officially cleared.

In cases where the E-I is officially cleared, it is important for the supervisor to address any lingering doubts or prejudices to help alleviate residual suspicion and E-I discomfort sooner than later. It is important for higher rank to do this, too.

CHAPTER 22

How All of This Gets Accomplished

1. Set an example—decide to <u>be</u> a professional manager. This means believing in and living the principles, values, expectations, and beliefs that define the role of the position you occupy. If you want respect from subordinates, you must respect them in kind. If you want them to trust you, then trust them, too. If you want employees to be dedicated to and hard working at their job, then dedicate yourself in a like manner. If you want them to be open and honest with you, then be open and honest with them. It's what you do and how you approach your job that sets the tenor of the workplace.

2. Treat everyone with respect, regardless of their position or relationship to you. It means avoiding nicknames, laughing at or tolerating improper jokes or actions of others, etc. It requires listening and taking subordinates' ideas and issues seriously. Avoid scoffing at or ignoring their concern(s). Respond with sincere attention and appreciation.

3. When correction is necessary, do it with the intent to resolve and correct as opposed to humiliate and punish. When discipline is necessary, make sure it is fair, impartial, procedural, and professional.

4 Ensure fairness through equal access to you and your daily approach to others. Avoid favoritism or disproportionate networking, etc. Remember the little things that put a human touch to the process *Look employees in the eye, soften your demeanor when necessary, listen with both ears, extend an occasional sincere thank you, maintain the awareness of and attention to significant events in employees' lives, i.e., promotions, birthdays, anniversaries, etc.* Show your employees that you care, and appreciate their work and commitment to the mission.

5 Address any kind of bias or discrimination, negative peer pressure, and interpersonal conflict right away with an added effort to address underlying causes.

6 Create and maintain avenues for an aggrieved employee to report and address wrongs, and ensure an unfettered freedom to do so.

The more one strives to keep a workplace professional, the less likely he or she will experience a significant employee problem. It will also help to ensure a stronger leadership position should one occur, and bolster it during any subsequent oversight or adjudication.

Remember: employees want to be respected and addressed civilly. They expect whoever occupies the position of first line supervisor to be competent, fair, and trustworthy, and to possess the courage to do what is right. It helps for the supervisor to believe in the nobility of the position he or she occupies, the importance of the public trust, a common purpose, and to accept, and appreciate that the job will get done through subordinates. All of this must be considered while you lead them through whatever challenges any kind of change will present.

Believe it, live it, and enjoy the ride …

Addendum

Gravity of circumstance

Circumstances surround everything we say, do, and encounter throughout the day. They are the why, where, when, historical contexts, implications, reactions, consequences, and sensitivities that exist around or extend from every act and utterance. There are aggravating, exigent, extenuating, and all kinds of special circumstances. While some are readily apparent, many remain hidden from those unable or unwilling to consider them. *Yes, it was a funny joke and everyone laughed, including you. However, what circumstances exist around the telling of the joke that could turn it into something other than what was intended?* A simple act or utterance can involve circumstances that propel it far beyond its original intent or expectation.

"Let me help you with that, boy!" While the intent may have been to help, the salutation of 'boy' could involve circumstances of greater gravity; the intent, which was directed at a young lad of similar ilk, can be seen as offensive to an adult of differing race or ethnicity. Major circumstances of racial or ethnic discrimination and insensitivity could come to bear, which most may not see. The intent may have been to help, but that one word, 'boy,' depending on the circumstances, could generate unexpected consequences of significant gravity.

The key to assessing any 'gravity of circumstance' lies in the ability to discern and comprehend the seriousness (gravity) of consequences that *could* or will impact what you are hearing, observing, or doing.

When planning a traffic checkpoint at a certain location, or engaging a particular investigative activity, one must look beyond the idea or plan and consider circumstances that could negatively impact the effort (risk of injury or offense to innocent third parties). Maybe the checkpoint location is good for catching violators, but the physical location poses a risk to other motorists. A planned crackdown on a certain activity is a good idea, but failing to inform or get community wide support creates circumstances that can undermine or defeat its worthy intent.

A picture of an off duty officer partially clothed and obviously intoxicated is anonymously posted on a bulletin board in a locker room as a joke meant for limited viewing. Does the inappropriate use of the bulletin board and/or the content of the photo bring to bear circumstances that would require something more than just removing and throwing it away? While the intent of the posting may have been innocuous, the circumstances surrounding it may change all that. *Maybe the pictured officer has been suspected of abusing alcohol, or the photo shows it occurred in the public's view. Would these circumstances require more attention on your part?* Here's where seeing what others may not comes into the equation.

While some may see an aggressive officer skirting proper procedure and protocol as an active and productive employee, circumstances of profiling, discrimination, abuse of power, and/or lack of discretion may dictate otherwise.

The point: Every new manager must get used to thinking more about circumstances surrounding what he/she says, does, and encounters, which now includes the responsibility for what others under their supervision say and do.

Bibliography

Books

Ayres, Richard M., J.D., Coderman, David S. Ph.D., *Leading to Make a Difference*. Fredericksburg, Virginia. Academy Leadership Associates LLC, 2011

Bennis, Warren, Nanus, Burt. Leaders: *The Strategy For Taking Charge*. Harper & Row, 1985

Bennis, Warren. *On Becoming a Leader*. Reading, MA. Addison-Wesley Publishing Co., 1989

Bennis, Warren, Thomas, Robert J. *Geeks & Geezers*, Boston,MA., Harvard Business Review, 2002

Bennett, William J., *Virtues of Friendship and Loyalty*, Nashville, Tennessee, W Publishing Group, 2001

Blanchard, Ken, O'Connor, Michael, *Managing by Values*. San Francisco, Berrett-Koehler Publisher, 1997

Blanchard, Kenneth, Peale, Norman Vincent, *The Power of Ethical Management*, New York, Fawcett Crest, 1988

Blanchard, Ken. Gottry, Steve, *The On-Time, On-Target Manager,* New York, HarperCollins Publishers, 2004

Blauner, Andrew, edited by, *COACH,* New York, Boston, Warner Books, 2005

Brinkman, Dr. Rick, Kirschner, Dr. Rick, *Dealing with People You Can't Stand,* New York, McGraw-Hill, 2002

Covey, Stephen R, *The 7 Habits of Highly Effective People,* New York, et al., Simon & Shuster, 1989

Covey, Stephen R., Merrill, Roger A, and Rebecca R. *First Things First.* New York, et al., Simon & Shuster, 1994

Delattre, Edwin J., *Character And Cops,* Washington, D.C., American Enterprise Institute for Public Policy Research, 1989

Emener, William G., Hutchinson, William S., Jr., Richard, Michael A., editors., *Employee Assistance Programs,* 3rd *edition,* Springfield, Illinois, Charles C. Thomas, Publisher, 2003

Felton, Eric. *Loyalty, the Vexing Virtue.* New York. Simon & Shuster, 2011.

Graff, Garrett M, *The Threat Matrix,* New York. Little, Brown and Company, 2011

Howard, Philip K., *The Death of Common Sense,* New York, Warner Books, 1994

Halle, Oliver G., *Taking the Harder Right,* Smyrna, Georgia, Concord Bridge Press, 2006

Homes, Robert L., *Basic Moral Philosophy,* 3rd Edition, Toronto, Canada, 2003

Jennings, Marianne J., J.D., *The Seven Signs of Ethical Collapse,* New York, St. Martin's Press, 2006

Lehr, Dick, *The Fence,* New York, HarperCollins, 2009

Lavin, James, *Management Secrets of the New England Patriots,* Stamford, Connecticut, Pointer Press, 2005

Mager, Robert F., Pipe, Peter, *Analyzing Performance Problems,* Atlanta, Georgia, Center for Effective Performance, Inc., 1997

Neat, James E., Jr., *The #1 Guide to Performance Appraisals,* Perrysburg, Ohio, Neal Publications, Inc., 2001

Paine, Lynn Sharp, *Value Shift,* New York, N.Y., McGraw Hill, 2003

Robinette, Hillary, *Burnout in Blue*, New York, N.Y., Praeger Publishers, 1987

Robbins, Stephen P., *The Truth About Managing People.* Upper Saddle River, N.J., Prentice Hall, 2003

Steingold, Fred S., *The Employer's Legal Handbook, 4th edition*, Berkeley, California, Nolo, 2002

Topchik, Gary S., *Managing Workplace Negativity*, New York, Amacom, 2001

Torre, Joe with Dreher, Henry, *Joe Torre's Ground Rules for Winners*, New York, Hyperion, 1999

Wilson, James Q., *The Moral Sense*, New York, The Free Press, a Division of Macmillan, Inc., 1993

Wilson, James Q., *Moral Judgment*, New York, Basic Books, a Divison of HarperCollins Publishers, 1997

Index

V

Value, The highest, 69
Values, 6, 51, 62
Verbal assault, 129
Vexing virtue, 83
Virtuous friend, 106
Vision, 11

W

Wallis Simpson, 144
Washington Redskins, 9
Whistle blower, 53, 61, 167-168
White lies, 74
Whitey Bulger, 98
Wilson, James Q, 103
Workplace violence, 133
Wrongs, words of, 56

www.ingramcontent.com/pod-product-compliance
Lightning Source LLC
Chambersburg PA
CBHW031219290326
41931CB00035B/301